Frederick Watson

The defenders of the faith; or, The Christian apologists of the second and third centuries

Frederick Watson

The defenders of the faith; or, The Christian apologists of the second and third centuries

ISBN/EAN: 9783337263270

Printed in Europe, USA, Canada, Australia, Japan

Cover: Foto ©Lupo / pixelio.de

More available books at **www.hansebooks.com**

DEFENDERS OF THE FAITH.

The Fathers for English Readers.

THE

DEFENDERS OF THE FAITH;

OR,

THE CHRISTIAN APOLOGISTS OF THE
SECOND AND THIRD CENTURIES.

BY

THE REV. F. WATSON, M.A.,

LATE FELLOW AND THEOLOGICAL LECTURER OF ST. JOHN'S COLLEGE,
CAMBRIDGE, AND RECTOR OF STARSTON, NORFOLK.

PUBLISHED UNDER THE DIRECTION OF THE TRACT COMMITTEE.

LONDON:
SOCIETY FOR PROMOTING CHRISTIAN KNOWLEDGE.
SOLD AT THE DEPOSITORIES:
77, GREAT QUEEN STREET, LINCOLN'S-INN FIELDS, W.C.;
4, ROYAL EXCHANGE, E.C.; 48, PICCADILLY, W.;
AND BY ALL BOOKSELLERS.
New York: Pott, Young, & Co.

WYMAN AND SONS, PRINTERS,
GREAT QUEEN STREET, LINCOLN'S INN FIELDS,
LONDON, W.C.

PREFACE.

THE aim of this book has been to combine together, in a connected form, and in a graphic manner, the main points of the arguments urged on behalf of the Christians by the numerous Apologists of the second and third centuries. Their writings have a considerable interest and importance for us, for it is from them we learn the moral and religious condition of the world at the coming of our Lord. They picture to us the faith, and hope, and patient endurance of the early Christians. In their time the Church and the world were open enemies, and they describe the bitter struggle which ended in the victory of the Church.

There is little in this book which has not been derived from the works of the Apologists themselves, and the Ecclesiastical History of Eusebius; but the author has also to express his obligations to the following books:—

Döllinger's 'Jew and Gentile in the Court of Christ.'
Lecky's 'European Morals.'
Blunt's 'History of the First Three Centuries.'

Westcott's 'History of the Canon of the New Testament.'

Neander's 'History of the Christian Church.' (The references are to Bohn's edition.)

It must also be stated that the translations of the passages quoted have been mainly derived from the translation of the ante-Nicene Fathers, published by T. & T. Clark, Edinburgh.

CONTENTS.

CHAPTER I.

THE ENEMIES OF THE FAITH . . . . *Page* 1

Early History of the Church not commonly known—Its interest to Christians—The Apologetic Period—Its characteristics—Its special difficulties—The four great opposing forces—Law, Reason, Interest, Superstition.

CHAPTER II.

EPOCHS IN THE STRUGGLE . . . . . *Page* 13

Picture I. The Commission—Picture II. The Gift of Power and the first Victory—Picture III. The struggle deepens and widens—Picture IV. The contempt of the world—Picture V. The rapid increase—Picture VI. The active opposition—Picture VII. The extension of the kingdom—Picture VIII. The pitched battle with the State—Picture IX. The last bitter struggle—Picture X. The triumph.

CHAPTER III.

THE DEFENDERS OF THE FAITH . . . *Page* 27

The Church's work; Conversion of souls—Edification of the faithful—Vindication of her position in the eyes of men.—Work of the Apologists—Its limits—The Apologetic period—Those addressed—The results of their writings—Their use to us.

CHAPTER IV.

THE DEFENCE . . . . *Page* 36

Charges.—Immorality; Basis of charge—Failure of the Investigations to procure evidence—In Bithynia—In Gaul.—Counter-evidence; The deaths of Christians—Reformation of life produced by Christianity—Nature of Christianity.—Suspicion caused by Gnostic Immorality—Charge never believed in by intelligent heathen.—Monstrous worship; the Christian's God supposed to be the head of an ass—The Cross—The God Serapis—The bodies of the martyrs.—Charge retorted by the Apologists.—Atheism; Reason for the charge—Its odium—The Christians reckoned to be responsible for the troubles of the times—Persecutions followed on calamities—The Apologetic answer—The times are not specially bad—The world is growing old—The Christians have a God whom they worship.—The political charge; Roman jealousy against secret societies—The Christian society likely to excite jealousy—Could not be tolerated—The Christians the cause of disturbances—The novelty of Christianity—The legal charge against the Christians—A Christian's trial—The question of the judge—A denial accepted—Confession followed by torture to compel denial—First legal recognition of Christianity.—Disloyalty to the Emperor; another King, one Jesus—The Christians could not worship the Emperor.—Unprofitableness of Christians to the State; Christianity all-absorbing—Charge denied, but some reason for it—Idolatry closely connected with every sphere of public life—Scruples as to the use of arms.

CHAPTER V.

THE ATTACK . . . . *Page* 71

Christianity intolerant—The truth of the heathen religion already given up—Heathenism maintained for political reasons—The gods vilified in the games and plays — The old Roman religion corrupted — Superstition still strong.—Objections against heathenism; Polytheism — Image-worship — Representation of the deities by images—History of the gods—No connection between Roman prosperity and the Roman religion—The heathen religion demon-worship—The demons, their nature and works—Subject to Christians.—The heathen philosophy; its slight results—Able to expose error, unable to discover truth —Scepticism of the age—Vices of philosophers—Philosophy not practical—Its contradictions—Its Exclusiveness—Stoic school a partial exception—Connection of philosophy with Christianity; Justin's view—Tertullian's view.

CHAPTER VI.

CHRISTIANS AND CHRISTIANITY . . . *Page* 98

The God of the Christians—God's Providence—The immortality of the soul and the resurrection of the body—Doctrines practical—Argument from analogy—Christian religion based on Christ—The wisdom and morality of His teaching—Confessed by heathen—Ancient prophecies—Indiscriminate use of prophecy by Apologists—Testimonies from Scripture out of place in an Apology—Christ's miracles ascribed to magic—Contrasted with the miracles of magicians — Purity of Christian lives—Heathen religion and morality not connected—Christian religion spiritual

—Firm endurance of persecutions—Christian love to their fellow-men—The Christian sacrifices—Lucian's account of the Christians—Celsus's account.

CHAPTER VII.

THE GREEK APOLOGISTS . . . . . . *Page* 127

Difference between the Greek and Latin Apologists; Time — Substance — Spirit. — Greek Apologists — Justin; his character—Studies in philosophy—Conversion—Active labours—Death—His first Apology—His Dialogue with Trypho.—Tatian; his heresy—his position—his former life—his view of the Greek religion and philosophy—Gnostic tendencies in his Apology.—Athenagoras; a philosopher—His conversion—His plea—Nothing in a name—The three charges—His defence—Its excellence.—Epistle to Diognetus; its occasion—Description of the world before Christ—Christ's coming—Its difference from other Apologies.—Theophilus; his conversion—His references to the Old Testament.—Clement of Alexandria; his Apology an exhortation—His invitation to the heathen to listen to the new song.—Origen; his Apology an answer to a particular work—Celsus's method of attack—Origen's defence.

CHAPTER VIII.

THE LATIN APOLOGISTS : . . . . . . *Page* 165

The Latin Apologists Africans — Tertullian; his Apology—Its force—Its inappropriate spirit—Its description of the Christian trials—Its answer to the charges of illegality—Immorality—Neglect of the gods—Parallel between the making of images and the persecuting of Christians—Profanity of the heathen towards their own gods—The God of the Christians Christ — Heathen hip the worship of demons—Christian power em—Roman prosperity disconnected from R ety—The Christians not traitors to the Empe nature of the Christian society—Distinction Christianity and philosophy—Appeal against n cruelty—Merits of Tertullian's apology.— ony of the Soul—Why useful—Whence de force.—Minucius Felix; a dialogue—Its Cæcilius's statement—All things doubtful—H useful—Christian doctrines foolish—Octavius —Nature declares God plainly—God's providen niversal—God one—God incomprehensible—Character of the heathen religion—Defence of the Christians against the charges of immorality and foolishness.—Cyprian; his description of Christian sufferings—Description of an exorcism—Arnobius; his standpoint—His speculations on the nature of the soul—His argument against material sacrifices.—Lactantius; his ambitious object—His criticisms of other Apologists—His refutation of philosophy—Conclusion.

PREFACE TO THE SERIES.

WHILE all those   retend to the character of educated people would b   ied to be ignorant of the history of Greece and Ro   ves and achievements of the great men of these count   the works of their chief writers, it is to be feared that   ntent themselves often with a very slight knowledge of the history of the Christian Church and of the illustrious ecclesiastics who have exercised so vast an influence upon the institutions and manners, the literature and philosophy, as well as the religion of modern Europe.

The series of volumes, of which the present forms a part, is intended to present to ordinary English readers Sketches of the Chief Fathers of the Church, their biographies, their works, and their times.

Those already prepared are—
    THE APOSTOLIC FATHERS,
    THE DEFENDERS OF THE FAITH (Apologists),
    ST. AUGUSTINE, and
    ST. JEROME.
Others are in preparation.

It is hoped that the series will supply the intelligent Churchman with a lively, accurate, and fairly complete view of the most important periods of Church history.

DEFENDERS OF THE FAITH.

CHAPTER I.

THE ENEMIES OF THE FAITH.

For one reason or another the views of most of us about the early history of the Christian Church are very indefinite. We read that history to the point where it is left in the Acts of the Apostles, and then we stop, and scarcely ask ourselves what became of the Apostles, or what became of the Church when the Apostles died. We know that the work went on; we know that that little seed, which, in the Bible narrative, we see sprouting, grew into the greatest of trees. We know that the growth of the Church was not easy or unchecked. We have read of the sufferings of the martyrs, and have learnt something of the cruel torments inflicted upon men, women, and children to cause them to deny their faith. But our notions are vague. We scarcely know why the Christians were persecuted, or how they defended themselves. We cannot tell the names of the champions of the faith in Apostolic times. We know something about Bible times, and we know something about Reformation times, but the intervening history is far too much of a blank to us. The Church was living and doing its work all that time. Why should we know nothing about it?

Now it is quite certain we lose very much by our ignorance. Do we want to be interested? By our ignorance we lose the most thrilling and beautiful stories. Do we want to be instructed? By our ignorance we lose the most noble examples, encouragements, and warnings. There is something in the early history of our Church—remember it is *ours*—which is likely above all things to fire us with noble purposes, and to inspire us with new zeal for the work we have in our generation to do. Why is it that we enjoy so much the fine old stories of English history, how Alfred defeated the Danes, and firmly established his kingdom, or Harold and his English stood firm against the Norman invader, and died for their country? Why is it that Edward I.'s wars with the Scots, and Edward III. and Henry V.'s wars with the French, interest us so much, and yet we care so little for the battles and the victories of the Christian Church? "I am an Englishman," you say, "and therefore it is that I am proud to hear what my brave English ancestors did in the olden days." You are quite right, but remember also you are a Christian—you belong not only to the English nation, but to the Christian Church. Listen, then, to the story of the noble deeds of your Christian ancestors. Oh, they were very brave! Oh, they were very patient! They won far nobler victories than Cressy or Agincourt. Your English ancestors, in days gone by, won for you freedom and a noble name, and you love them. Your Christian ancestors won for you a still greater freedom and a still nobler name. Will you not love them too? You read how the arrows came clouding the air, and the horsemen came rushing headlong to crush the little army of English who stood all firm and undaunted, and who, though few, said that they did not ask for reinforcements, they were enough to conquer, and they were enough to die. They stood in their ranks, they fell bravely, they triumphed nobly, and we are proud of them. But oh! be proud also of that army which is fighting still, and to which you yourself belong, "who through faith subdued kingdoms . . . . waxed valiant in fight, and turned to flight the armies of the aliens."[1] Remember they suffered, and so you have not to suffer; they laboured, and you have entered into their labours; you are fighting the same battle and under the same banner; they have won the victory, and you must win the victory in the same way. Will it not be well for you then to inquire into their history, so that you may learn who were their enemies, and what were their weapons, and where were their battlefields, and why they fought, and how they fought, and how in God's strength they won the victory? And now the subject of this book has been pretty clearly stated. It is to tell you the story of the battles of the Christian Church, and the champions of the Christian faith, in early times. For the most part we shall confine ourselves to the second and third centuries A.D.

[1] Hebrews xi. 33, 34.

Occasionally there will be something to say about the first century, and once or twice we shall have to go a little way into the fourth; but for the most part we shall be concerned only with the time extending from 100 A.D. to 300 A.D.

Now there are two things specially to notice about this period. The first is, the Apostles were then all dead, and those who succeeded them had not the same outward tokens of God's presence. The preachers of the Gospel were not able, generally at least, to heal the bodies of men, and so their task was in some respects far more difficult, and a hearing was not so easily obtained by them. The second thing to notice is, that all this while the rulers of the state were heathen, and therefore more or less opposed to Christianity. Constantine was the first Christian emperor, and he did not come into his power till the year 312 A.D. So you see, during this period, on the one hand, some of the help God had hitherto given the Church was taken away, and on the other, she had difficulties to contend against which were afterwards removed. This was the time of the hardest struggle of the Christian Church; this was the time also when her most brilliant victories were gained; this was the time, it is not too much to say, the battle of The Faith was won.

And now to proceed to my subject. When the last surviving Apostle died, only a beginning of the great work which Christ had entrusted to His Church had been made. At the end of the first century, the Christians were only a feeble folk. The world was just beginning to know about them. So far as they were known, they were hated much, but despised more. The Roman Empire was already feeling jealous about them, as people who might one day be troublesome; it was soon about to try to put them down. As we may say, the two armies—the army for Christ and the army against Him—were then being put in array, army against army. The one army was like " two little flocks of kids,"[1] but the other filled the whole earth. If you looked on the one side you saw nobody of any importance; at the present day we scarcely know more than half a dozen of their names. We may safely say that there were very few of noble birth, very few who were wise with worldly wisdom, very few indeed who had, as far as men could see, any qualifications for the task of overcoming the world. They belonged mostly to the most despised nation of the world, and that nation had cast them out of her bosom. The Jews, persecuted by all others, were themselves persecutors of the Christians.

And then, on the other side, what was there? There was the whole world; and a world united under one man, who ruled it according to his own will and pleasure. Such was his power, such the reverence he received, that more than human honours were paid him; even whilst living he was worshipped as a god.

Now, this concentration of power under one head added greatly to the difficulties of the Church. Other great movements have, in their infancy and weakness, profited greatly by the fact that sovereignty was shared

---

[1] 1 Kings xx. 27.

by many kingdoms, commonly rivals, and jealous of one another. Political necessities have often produced the strangest combinations, and the most unexpected results. At the worst of times, the authority of a State could not extend beyond its own limits; and hence those persecuted in one city would flee into another. But the Church owed its victory to no such external circumstances; in those early times there was but one State and one ruler of it. The law said, "The Christians ought not to be"; and the magistrates, when required, had *always* to enforce the law. And when the emperor said, as he *sometimes* did by a special edict, Put that law into force; there was then no one to be their defender, no land to which they could fly for refuge, no political combinations which could stay the persecuting hand. And thus the Christians, without any earthly defender, had to contend against the whole force of the *Law;* they had to withstand the united force of the great Roman Empire with its Emperor-god.

But this was not all; all the *wise* men of the world were against them. The philosophers of that day were, for the most part, men without religion and without morality. They were too wise to believe in the old heathen gods, but they were not wise enough to attain to the knowledge of the one true God. They were able, some of them, to lay down excellent rules of life, but few thought it necessary to put them into practice. They were proud and self-sufficient, and looked down with contempt upon the unlearned and ignorant common people. The Christians were, for the most part, unlearned and uneducated; and yet, notwithstanding their deficiencies in philosophic training and intellectual qualifications, they dared to speak authoritatively on matters concerning which the wisest teachers professed their ignorance. The philosophers had pulled down many religions in their time; they were foes to all superstitions, and now they banded together to pull down what they considered to be the last and worst of all. And thus the leaders of Thought joined the rulers of the State in the battle against the Christian name. The force of *Reason* was added to the force of *Law*.

To these two a more popular and widely-reaching force was added—the force of *Interest*. It is marvellous to see how closely intertwined were the heathen religion and all that concerned the outer life of a man and the administration of the State. The religion of a man had little or nothing to do with his thoughts or affections, and it exercised little or no influence over his morals; but it entered into every relation and action of his family and public life. When you were born, when you were married, and when you died, gods had to be propitiated, lest they should do you harm, and in order that they might do you good. At the corners of the streets, and at the doors of the houses, in the halls, and in the bedchambers, at every turn one might say, images met your eye. There was no occupation over which some god did not preside, no public festival without its religious sacrifices, no act of business without its idolatrous ceremonies. It followed, of course, that there were thousands of people who got their living from the idolatrous worship; and therefore thousands of people who were most anxious that the old heathen customs should be kept up. Very early we see the force of interest exerted against Christianity. "By this craft we have our wealth,"[1] said Demetrius to the makers of silver shrines for Diana. By Paul's preaching, "this our craft is in danger to be set at nought."[2] The fear of such a result was sufficient, as we know; forthwith the craftsmen stirred up the people. Similarly, Pliny (A.D. 100 circa), Governor of Bithynia, noticed that in his province there was no demand for the sacrificial victims; in consequence, he ordered an inquiry, and ultimately a persecution. It was of direct importance to the Government that the temples should be well attended; when they were deserted their revenues declined.[3] By the advance of Christianity, the priests lost their profits and their influence, the armies their soldiers, the lawyers their clients, the taverns their customers, and the sculptors and painters their patrons.[4] All the artists and craftsmen derived the better part of their gains from the requirements of the heathen religion. And besides the temples and their gods there were also the shows and the games. The Christians could not join in the idolatry of the one, they dared not come in contact with the pollutions of the other. The hangers-on at the shows were only less numerous and various than those at the temples; and thus we see the contingent to the army against Christ, collected under

---

[1] Acts xix. 25.　　[2] Ib. xix. 27.　　[3] Tert. Apol. c. 42.
[4] Cf. for this Blunt's 'Three Centuries,' pp. 144, 145.

the banner of Interest, was very large. With intense bitterness all these men banded themselves together against a religion, which deprived them not only of the gods which they worshipped but of the food which they ate. And thus to the force of *Law* and *Reason* was added the force of *Interest*.

To these three forces, strong as they were, yet another, perhaps the strongest of all, was added—the force of *Superstition*.

The philosophers might have sneered to their heart's content; those who earned a livelihood from idolatry or the public games might have grumbled; but the State and the powers of the law would have been indifferent; had it not been that the common people rose with one voice and said, "Away with these fellows from the earth, for it is not meet that they should live." In most of the persecutions of the 2nd century, it was the people, not the State authorities, which took the initiative. No doubt interested agitators were behind the scenes, but the popular fury was, beyond all, the persecuting force. The order of proceedings commonly was, first, popular risings against the Christians, and then, proceedings against them according to the forms of law. Very often the Emperor and the provincial governors were their best friends. Trajan discouraged anonymous informations.[1] Hadrian said the Christians were not to be arrested on mere popular clamour.[2] Antoninus Pius strongly disapproved of the violent proceedings of the mob.[2] Aurelius says the Christians must be punished with

[1] Trajan's Letter to Pliny.
[2] Cf. Neander, 'History of the Church,' pp. 140, 143.

divers tortures yet so that justice is mingled.[1] The governors also *sometimes* did not fear the people,[2] and contrived means of dismissing the Christians unpunished. Certainly of all the enemies of the Church the people were the most bitter and violent. Tertullian[3] tells us that none more frequently than the rabble demanded the lives of the Christians. "How often," he says, "does the hostile mob, paying no regard to you (*i.e.* the authorities), take the law into its own hand, and assail us with stones and flames!"

And the reason of this appears to be quite plain. It was their *Superstition* which urged the people on. We must remember that the heathen religion was an elaborate plan for securing national prosperity. The sacrifices were bribes to secure the favour of the gods, or rather, perhaps, magic spells to compel them to act according to the sacrificer's wish.[4] If everything was done properly, without a mistake in the prayer of consecration, or the occurrence of a sight or sound of ill omen at the time of sacrificing, or a defect in the entrails of the victim, then the wished-for result was sure to be secured, the god was compelled to be propitious.[5] Of course it followed that times of difficulty, danger, or calamity, were times for special vows and sacrifices. Generals uttered vows just before joining battle with the enemy. A pestilence filled the temples with devout worshippers. The idea

---

[1] Cf. Neander, 'History of the Church,' p. 149.
[2] Tert. ad Scapulam, c. 4.
[3] Apol. c. 37.   [4] Döllinger's 'Jew and Gentile,' p. 75.
[5] Döllinger's 'Jew and Gentile,' p. 77.

in many minds, at such a time, was, the gods, one or all, are angry because we have neglected them; if we only sacrifice largely enough, prosperity will return. The expense incurred by the State on these sacrifices for national prosperity was very great. Sometimes it was so difficult to get sacrifices that representations in bread or wax took the place of the animals themselves. As many as three hundred bulls were offered in one sacrifice to one god. At the death of Tiberius and at Caligula's accession to the throne, upwards of 160,000 victims were sacrificed. Augustus and Marcus Aurelius used so many beasts, that it was said all oxen and calves hoped that the emperors might never return from their journeys or campaigns, as otherwise they would be infallibly lost.[1]

It so happened that in the 2nd and 3rd centuries there was a constant succession of calamities in the State. There were "famines, and pestilences, and earthquakes." "The gods are angry" was the general cry. "These calamities have fallen upon us because their shrines are neglected; we must propitiate them with sacrifices." They did so. But there were many gaps in the line of worshippers; the Christians absented themselves. By them were addressed no supplications, by them were offered no gifts of expiation to the angry gods. Then the popular anger burst forth in uncontrollable fury. "It is because of those impious Christians," they said, "that we are suffering all these troubles. Away with them to the lion."

---

[1] For all this see Döllinger's 'Jew and Gentile,' p. 80.

At such times the Christians suffered without trial at all. Although the magistrates might scoff at popular superstition, they quailed before the popular wrath. They might expostulate, but when they saw that they prevailed nothing and that rather a tumult was made, they let the people have their own way. They put the existing law in force against men for whom they cared nothing, and who in their opinion deserved punishment for being so obstinate and troublesome.

And thus we see that these four forces, *Law*, *Reason*, *Interest*, and *Superstition*, were all combined against the disciples of Christ. The learned few and the superstitious many, the law administrators and the lawless mob, those who reckoned the heathen religion to be the great support of the State power and those who knew that it gave them support and subsistence, the priests and philosophers, the kings and people, all hated the name of Christ, and all at times combined together to give His Church a crushing blow. The heathen raged, the people imagined a vain thing; "the kings of the earth stood up, and the rulers were gathered together against the Lord and against His Christ." And what was the result? He that dwelleth in heaven laughed them to scorn; the Lord had them in derision. He said, "*I* have set my King on my holy hill of Zion." He fulfilled His promise, "Ask of me and I shall give Thee the heathen for Thine inheritance, and the uttermost parts of the earth for Thy possession."

CHAPTER II.

EPOCHS IN THE STRUGGLE.

In the last chapter a description was given of the enemies against which the early Christians had to fight. This chapter is intended to describe, in a series of separate pictures, various epochs in the struggle.

PICTURE I.

A few men and women are assembled in an upper room in a house at Jerusalem. The number of their names is about one hundred and twenty. Their Lord and Master has just been taken up from them into heaven. He has left them His charge, and it is this: "All power is given unto me in heaven and in earth. Go ye, therefore, and teach all nations, baptizing them in the name of the Father, and of the Son, and of the Holy Ghost: teaching them to observe all things whatsoever I have commanded you: and, lo, I am with you alway, even unto the end of the world. Amen."[1]

According to the instructions given, they are tarrying in the city of Jerusalem for the promise of the Father of which Jesus had told them. They

---

[1] Matt. xxviii. 18, 19, 20.

continue in prayer and supplication, and they are waiting for the signal to go forth and conquer the world.

PICTURE II.

The time of waiting is over, and the day of work and conflict has begun. The Day of Pentecost is running its course. The promise has been fulfilled, "I will pour out my Spirit upon all flesh." The Church fights its first battle, and wins its first victory. "The same day there are added unto them about three thousand souls."

PICTURE III.

Now comes a time when the struggle widens and deepens.

At first the battle-ground is Jerusalem, and the Church's chief enemy the Jews. Then persecution disperses Christ's soldiers into many different countries. Unlike the armies of the World, dispersion increases the power of the army of the Cross. One single soldier of Christ is able to seize and hold a position for his Lord. Still hatred and opposition follow them wherever they go. The Jews will not believe, and stir up the Gentiles. The Gentiles complain that these men are turning the world upside down. Men can no longer ignore the infant Church. To the period of insignificance succeeds one of ever-increasing hatred.

Forty years pass away. The testimony of the Jews now is, "This sect is everywhere spoken against."[1]

[1] Acts xxviii. 22.

And as for the Gentiles, the Emperor Nero, having set fire to Rome, wants a scapegoat on which to lay his own crimes, and he finds the Christians ready to his hand. Now comes the first great sowing of the seed-blood of the Christians. They are crucified. They are sewn up in the skins of wild beasts and thrown to the dogs. Their garments are smeared with pitch, and they are set on fire to light up the public gardens. The people think they suffer unjustly; they believe them to be guiltless of the crime ascribed to them; but after all they are guilty of hatred of the human race, and they are odious for their crimes.[1]

PICTURE IV.

Still as yet the Roman Government hardly deems the Christians worthy of its notice, and has, certainly, not the remotest conception what they are aiming at.[2] A jealous tyrant, Domitian, is on the throne, and he hears the Christians are setting up a kingdom. He inquires who is to be the king. He is told about David and David's throne, and about Christ the son of David. Then he seizes the grandsons of Judas, called the brother of our Lord; he thinks they must be David's heirs and Christ's heirs. They are brought before him to be examined. They are simple, rude men, not the sort of stuff out of which conspirators or pretenders to thrones are made. He finds they have a little farm which they cultivate with their own hands. They have the strong bodies and the hard hands of

---

[1] Tacitus, Annals, xv. 44.   [2] Eusebius, H.E. iii. 20.

tillers of the soil. He asks them about the kingdom they are setting up, and finds that it is spiritual and angelic, and that it will appear at the end of the world. When he hears this he is too contemptuous to make a reply; he sends them away as fools beneath his jealousy or his notice.

PICTURE V.

A very few years later, and the Church, working secretly, has so prospered as to excite the attention of the Roman governor of Bithynia. He finds the temples deserted. He is told few now buy victims for the sacrifices. The "contagious superstition" (that is his name for Christianity) is not confined to the cities only, it has spread to the villages. Many of all ranks and ages, and of both sexes, are infected. Persecution involves so many that he feels himself obliged to refer the matter to the Emperor. Although the measures he adopts have some success, the crime extends even during the persecution, and seems likely to extend still further.

A little later still, and the martyr Justin says that, wide as is the dispersion of the Jews, wider still is the dispersion of the Gospel of Christ. "There is not one single race of men, whether Barbarians or Greeks, or whatever they may be called, whether nomads or vagrants, or herdsmen living in tents, amongst whom prayers and giving of thanks are not offered through the name of the crucified Jesus."[1]

---

[1] Justin Martyr, Dialogue with Trypho, c. 117.

PICTURE VI.

Do you think the Christians spread because nobody opposed them? Look at this picture, painted by those who were engaged in the conflict.[1] It is to be found in a letter which begins thus: "The servants of Christ dwelling in Vienne and Lyons of Gaul to our brethren of Asia and Phrygia, who have the same faith and hope of redemption with us. Peace, grace, and glory be to you from God the Father and Christ Jesus our Lord."

This is their account—

"The greatness, indeed, of the tribulation, and the extent of the madness exhibited by the heathen against the saints, and the sufferings which the blessed martyrs endured, we are not able fully to declare, nor is it indeed possible to describe them. For the adversary assailed us with his whole strength, giving us already a foretaste how unbridled his future movements among us would be. And indeed he resorted to every means to accustom and exercise his own servants against those of God, so that we should not only be excluded from houses, and baths, and markets, but everything belonging to us was prohibited from appearing in any place whatever. But the grace of God contended for us, and rescued the weak, and prepared those who, like firm pillars, were able, through patience, to sustain the whole weight of the enemy's violence against him. These came to close quarters with them, enduring every species of reproach and torture. Making light of grievous trial,

[1] Eusebius, H.E. v. 1.

they hastened to Christ, showing in reality that 'the sufferings of this present time are not worthy to be compared with the glory that shall be revealed in us.' And first, they nobly sustained all the evils that were heaped upon them by the populace, clamours and blows, plunderings and robberies, and whatsoever a savage mob delight to inflict upon its enemies. After this they were led to the forum; and when they had been interrogated by the tribune and the authorities of the city in the presence of the multitude, they were shut up in prison until the arrival of the governor."

This, be it remembered, is but the beginning of the persecution—the prelude of infinitely worse things. But it is quite enough to convince us that the Christians had to face most violent opposition, and patiently to endure the bitterest trials.

PICTURE VII.

What is the result? Tertullian says, thirty years after, "The more we are mown down by you, the more in number we grow; the blood of the Christians is seed."[1] And again—"We are but of yesterday, and have filled every place among you; we leave nothing to you but the temples of your gods."[2] Christ's kingdom has already extended further than any kingdom of the world. Solomon, he observes, reigned only from Beersheba to Dan. Darius had not power over *all* nations. The Egyptians alone acknowledged the rule of Pharaoh. Nebuchadnezzar and Alexander had boundaries to their kingdoms. The Germans are enclosed within their territory. The sea shuts in

[1] Tert. Apol. c. 50.   [2] Ib. c. 37.

the Britons. The Moors are kept in bounds by the Romans. The Romans cannot extend their empire amongst the Barbarians. "But Christ's name is extended everywhere, and believed everywhere, and worshipped by all these nations. Everywhere He reigns, everywhere He is adored, everywhere He is imparted equally to all."[1]

PICTURE VIII.

Fifty years later, and after a long period of rest to the Church, the Roman State determines that it will put the Christians down. It has, meanwhile, gone so far at times as to show a benevolent neutrality towards them, though more often it has been hostile. One emperor has tacitly acknowledged that the Christians ought to be allowed to exist, and has decided that a piece of ground would be more fitly occupied by a Christian church than by a pastry-cook's shop. Mostly, the emperors have moderated the rigour of the laws and the fury of the people. But now the State awakes to the fact that the contest with Christianity is a matter of life and death—that if it does not put the Christians down, they will put it down. So the first systematic effort to suppress Christianity is made. Every citizen has, on a given day, to appear before the magistrates and offer sacrifices to the gods. It seems as if the Christian army would hardly have won this battle had it not been relieved. During the time of peace many soldiers, fit only for peace, had been added to the ranks.[2]

---

[1] Tert. c. Judæos, c. 7.   [2] Cyp. de Lapsis, c. 5.

Alexandria and Carthage are the chief battle-fields of which we have a record. In Alexandria[1] popular disturbances precede the imperial edict. A prophet appears who incites the people to do their gods service by slaying the Christians. Aged men and women are torn in pieces. Houses are plundered. No Christian dare show his face in the streets. The decree is promulgated; on a certain day all Christians are publicly to offer sacrifice to the heathen gods. Then the hearts of the faithful fail them, and it is feared that, if possible, even the elect will stumble. A widespread apostasy follows. To some their conspicuous position, to others their office in the State, was the stumbling-block. Fear overcame the constancy of some; friends over-persuaded others. The day appointed by the decree arrived. The roll-call was made. Some came up pale and trembling, amidst the jeers of the bystanders, afraid either to sacrifice or die. Others, more bold in their apostasy, denied they had ever been Christians. Some fled away. Others endured imprisonment and even torture for a while, and then apostatized. And there was a faithful remnant, firm and blessed pillars of the Lord, strengthened by Him, and receiving from Him strength proportioned to their mighty faith, who became marvellous witnesses of His kingdom.

At Carthage the state of things was very similar.[2] There were many different kinds of apostates.[3] Those who sacrificed; those who, by fraud and the con-

---

[1] Eus. H. E. vi. 41.   [2] Cyprian de Lapsis, c. 6.
[3] Cyp. Ep. 30.

nivance of the magistrate, obtained, without sacrificing, a certificate (libellum) that they had; those who said they had sacrificed and had got a certificate, having none; and those who allowed others to lie for them. There were those, also, thanks be to God, who endured to the end.

For the elects' sake, whom He had chosen, God shortened these days. Had it not been so, it seems as if the hopes of the enemy would have been realized, and Christianity been crushed. Tidings out of the East and the North troubled Decius, and soon he came to his end. The persecution did not outlast him long, and ten years afterwards Christianity was, for the first time, acknowledged to be a lawful religion of the Roman State.

PICTURE IX.

One last bitter conflict with the powers of the State ; and then, in a certain sense, the kingdoms of the world became the kingdoms of our Lord and of His Christ.

On February 22nd, 303, the storm, long hovering, burst. The Emperor Diocletian is over-persuaded by his colleague Galerius to crush that *imperium in imperio*—the Christian Church. The cathedral church of Nicomedia is broken open, and its Bibles and office-books are burnt; the building is first ransacked, and then hewn to the ground. The next day an imperial edict appears. All churches are to be levelled to the ground—all sacred books are to be burnt. Christian officials are to lose their places and all their civil rights—private Christians are to become slaves.

Then comes a time when, throughout the Empire, Bibles are burnt, churches are destroyed, and the prisons are full of priests; a time when Christian men are tortured with incredible horrors, and Christian women are sent to the brothels, and vile blasphemies are forged and circulated against the name of Christ. "The men bore fire, sword, and crucifixions, savage beasts, and the depths of the sea, the maiming of limbs, and searing with red-hot irons, pricking and digging out the eyes, and mutilation of the whole body, moreover, hunger, and mines, and prisons. And in all they exhibited a brave endurance for the sake of religion, rather than transfer that veneration and worship which are due to God only, to idols. The women also, no less than the men, were strengthened by the doctrine of the Divine Word; so that some endured the same trials as the men, and bore away the same prizes of excellence. Some, when forced away, yielded up their lives rather than submit to the violation of their bodies."[1]

Then was the boast made that the Christian name was destroyed, and the worship of the gods restored.[2] Then did the heathen rejoice in bounteous harvests, and settled peace, and a healthy air, and a calm sea, and a serene sky; all visible tokens, as they thought, that the gods were once more propitious to an empire at length separated from pollution and impiety.[3]

.The boasting was idle, and the gleam of prosperity delusive.[4] Famine, pestilence, and war desolated the

---

[1] Eusebius, H. E. viii. 14.
[2] See the inscriptions found at Clunia in Spain.
[3] Eus. H. E. ix. 7.   [4] Ib. ix. 8.

Empire at once. The only alleviation to these troubles was the conduct of the Christians. They only, in these distressing circumstances, exhibited sympathy and humanity. By them the famishing were fed, and the dead were buried. The fact was cried abroad, and men glorified the Christians' God. The Emperor, so lately the blasphemer of Christ and of Christians, completely changed his policy, and said persecution was a mistake he had never intended, and he granted full freedom of worship, and ordered the churches to be rebuilt, and the confiscated property to be restored.[1]

Nevertheless, the historian tells us,[2] vengeance from God quickly overtook him. Whilst his army was overthrown in the battle-field, he perished miserably at home. And in his dying agony he confessed that he suffered justly for his wanton excesses against the Christians.

PICTURE X.

Now for our last scene. The persecutors are dead. The Roman Empire has owned itself vanquished. On the banners of the army—once idolatrous signs—is to be seen the sign of Christ. Under the banner of the Cross the Romans now go forth to victory. The Emperor rebuilds and beautifies Christian churches, and he causes copies of the Scriptures to be made. He commands all the people of the East to honour the Christian religion, and to worship the one true God, whose power endureth for ever.[3]

[1] Eus. H. E. ix. 9.   [2] Ib. ix. 10.
[3] Sozomen, H. E. i. 8.

Then troubles inside the Christian Church arise. Constantine, the Emperor, is greatly distressed. He knows his own inability to mend matters, and he determines to summon a meeting of those who can, viz., the bishops of the Church. So, at the command of the Emperor, in conveyances provided by him, the most eminent of the ministers of God in all the Churches which had filled Europe, Africa, and Asia, were gathered together.[1]

One single building contained, by representation, the Syrians and the Cilicians, the Phœnicians and the Arabians, the Palestinians, the Egyptians, the Thebans, the Libyans, and the dwellers in Mesopotamia. Persia had its representative, nor was a Scythian lacking. Pontus and Galatia, Pamphylia, Cappadocia, Asia, and Phrygia, supplied the most distinguished representatives of all. Besides these there met together, Thracians and Macedonians, Achæans and Epirots, and those who lived at a greater distance still. Spain sent Hosius, Bishop and Confessor. Rome sent two priests to represent her aged bishop. The three other Apostolic thrones, Antioch, Jerusalem, and Alexandria, were represented by their bishops in person. Of bishops the total number was 318, and of attendant priests, and deacons, and acolytes, the number was beyond count. It was indeed a distinguished and august assembly, such as the world had never seen.[2] Some of them, says Eusebius, were eminent for their wisdom; some for the austerity of

---

[1] Soc. H. E. i. 7, 8.
[2] Life of Constantine, iii. 7—9; Socrates, Hist. Eccl. i. 8.

their life and patient endurance of persecution; and some for their modesty. Some were venerable for their age; and some rejoiced in the vigour of their youth. As another historian puts it, "Some were richly endowed with apostolical gifts, and many bore in their bodies the marks of the Lord Jesus Christ."[1]

Into that assembly, summoned, conveyed, and supported by himself, the Emperor Constantine enters.[2] He leaves his heathen attendants at the door. All rise to receive him, but he waits permission to take his seat. When he has taken his place, all present take theirs. Then he tells them his desire. It is to promote the unity of the Church. He reckons disunion therein to be an evil more terrible and more grievous than any kind of war. He trusts they will banish all causes of dissension, so as to accomplish a work most agreeable to God, and thus cause him, their fellow-servant, infinite joy. Then he leaves them to accomplish unimpeded a task in which he has no share.

And thus we see Christ has conquered. Kings have begun to bow down before Him; all nations have begun to do Him service. The Roman Empire has succumbed before the power of the Christian Church. Not, indeed, that the work of Christ's Church is accomplished; far from it. Her victory is far more apparent than real. But she has won her position in the world. Henceforward the Church and the State will be no longer open enemies. Nay, the State will take the Church under its protection, and the edicts of emperors will enforce the decisions of

---

[1] Theodoret, Hist. Eccl. i. 7.   [2] Soc. Hist. Eccl. i. 8.

bishops. But the victories which statecraft and state-power will gain will not be so pure and holy, not so real and lasting, as those which were won by the Divine power of the Truth. The State has gained an outward garb of Christianity, but the Church has now a source of corruption within. She has not, in times gone by, feared those who killed the body. She will have, in years to come, to fear evils which kill the soul, and which destroy her life.

In this book we have nothing to do with these later times. We have to do with a period when the Church won her victories against the State, and not by the aid of the State. Never, as it seems, was there a time when the Church's triumphs could be more fairly ascribed to the unassisted truth. The Christians of the second and third centuries had not seen Christ or His Apostles, and yet they believed, and spread their belief far and wide. They had not, commonly at any rate, the power of working miracles on the bodies of men, and yet they worked a miraculous change on their souls. All the powers of the world were arrayed against them, and this was the victory which overcame it—even their Faith.

CHAPTER III.

THE DEFENDERS OF THE FAITH.

How was the mighty work accomplished? That is the next question we have to discuss. Of course Christians are quite ready with their answer. The words of our hymn come into our mind at once. We think of the great army with its blood-red banner, and *Christ at the head.* We picture our soldiers conquering by suffering and death, through His help.

> Mocked, imprisoned, stoned, tormented,
> Sawn asunder, slain with sword,
> They have conquered Death and Satan
> By the might of Christ the Lord.

" By the might of Christ the Lord." Yes, that was the secret of the triumph of the Church over the world. Christ was in her; hence her might and hence her victory. The Divine Life in the Church was not more real in Apostolic times than after they had long fallen on sleep. Christ's promise remained firm, " Lo, I am with you alway, even unto the end of the world," and therefore was the victory won.

But this answer though true is not complete. " By the might of Christ the Lord " has been the secret of the triumph of the Church in all ages of her history, whether Apostolic, Primitive, Mediæval, or Modern. Yet, as we know, Christ's might has been manifest in many different ways. So we have still our question to answer. We want to know *how* the Divine energy was exerted—what human means was employed for the great end.

The Church of Jesus Christ had in early times, as in the present day, many different works, and many different kinds of workmen.

Her great work then, as now, was *the conversion of souls.* This was done, not so much by the reading as by the telling of the Gospel story.[1] Teachers were many, but books were few. This oral teaching was given not to great assemblies, but to individuals. Persecution soon put a stop to public preaching. And the way the Christians gained a hearing and a credence for this individual teaching was not so much by the power of working miracles, though some seem to have had it; nor by their pure and holy lives, though that too attracted attention; the Christians gained more hearers by their deaths than by their miracles or by their lives.[2] As the grass from the mowing, so sprung up the Christians with fresh vigour when cut down.[3] From the scene of terrible suffering patiently borne, the heathen went away predisposed to learn the source of such a mighty power of endurance, and to listen to the story of the Cross. It was felt

---

[1] Still notice that many of the Apologists were converted by the reading of the Scriptures.

[2] Tert. ad Scapulam, c. 5; Justin, Apol. ii. 12, 13.

[3] Tert. Apol. c. 50.

that such heroes must be in possession of a secret of strength hidden from the rest of the world.

The next work of the Church was to *build up souls in the most Holy Faith.* This was done in the secret assemblies for worship, which met at dead of night, and which were liable at any moment to be surprised, and, as a matter of fact, were often surprised by the authorities and the Roman soldiers.[1] With their lives in their hands, the Christians came to these to be made partakers of Christ by the ministry of the Word and Sacraments. At these was the reading of the Scriptures, prayer, thanksgiving, giving of alms, instruction and exhortation, administration of the Sacraments[2]—in early times the Agape or Love Feast.

But the Church had a work beyond the extension of her borders and the intensifying of the Divine Life within her members. *She had to vindicate her position in the eyes of men.* It was necessary to put before the world generally, and the State authorities particularly, what Christianity really was. Christianity was a *new* religion, in length of duration it could not compare with the religions of the gods and of the nations.[3] It was a *strange* religion, quite differing in kind from any other, without temples, images, altars, or sacrifices,[4] or at least any that could be seen.[5] It was a *secret* religion,[6] the assemblies were at night,

---

[1] Tert. Apol. c. 7.
[2] Justin Martyr, Apol. i. 65-67 ; Tert. Apol. c. 39.
[3] Ep. ad Diognetum, c. 1 ; Arnobius adv. Gentes, ii. 67, 69.
[4] Origen c. Celsum, vii. 62.   [5] Octavius, c. 10.
[6] Octavius, c. 8, 9.

and none but its baptized members were admitted to them.[1] It was a religion *spreading every day amongst all classes*, but especially amongst the women, the ignorant, and the criminal.[2] It was a religion *against which accusations of the most serious kind were made ;* the Christians were accused of being grossly immoral,[3] atheists,[4] traitors to the Emperor and the State,[5] and unprofitable citizens.[6] Even if these charges were not true, they could not be acquitted of incredible folly and of being led away by a wild enthusiasm.[7]

It was evidently quite necessary that these charges should be refuted. The Christians were bound to remove all these preliminary obstacles in the way of their success. Before the heathen could be converted to the faith of Christ, they had to be convinced that the Christians were not immoral, or atheists, or traitors. They had to be shown that at least there was some ground for Christian hope, and some excuse for what seemed to be incredible folly. So a class of men arose commonly called Apologists, that is to say, Defenders of the Faith, who made it their business to give the unconverted heathen some true notion of Christianity, to give them just that superficial view which an unbeliever was capable of taking. Strike, if strike you must, say these men to the heathen, but hear us first. Do not exterminate us from off the

---

[1] Just. Apol. i. 65, 66.
[2] Origen c. Celsum, iii. 44, 49; Justin Martyr, Dialogue, c. 117.
[3] Tert. Apol. c. 7, 39; Octavius, c. 9.
[4] Athenagoras, Plea, c. 3, 4.   [5] Tert. Apol. c. 29, 35.
[6] Tert. Apol. c. 42.   [7] Octavius, c. 8, 12.

face of the earth till you know a little more about us.¹ Do not be so unjust as to condemn us unheard.² You punish us simply for being Christians, but surely there is nothing in a mere name.³ You have vague ideas we are very wicked people, but you are mistaken, our lives are pure, we worship God, and we are loyal to the Emperor. Such was the work of the Defenders of the Faith; their object is not to teach truth, but to prepare the way for teaching. They do not prove that Christianity is true, they only prove that it is not utterly unreasonable or noxious. They remove stumbling-blocks and excite curiosity. In consequence, they rarely quote the Holy Scriptures. They refer to them, of course, constantly. They speak of their antiquity as extending far beyond all other books. They remark on their purity, contrasting them in this respect with the legends concerning the heathen gods. They describe their harmony and simplicity, contrasting them here with the hard and contradictory utterances of the philosophers. They assert the fulfilment of prophecies of undoubted antiquity, in the life of Christ and the establishment of His religion. But they do not appeal to them as authoritative. The heathen, for the most part, had never seen them, and if they had, did not believe in them. The Apologies are written to conciliate enemies, and so the arguments are such as he would allow.

The Apologists, or Defenders of the Faith, are then men living in the 2nd and 3rd centuries, who give the

---

[1] Tert. Apol. c. 1, 3.   [2] Just. Apol. ii. c. 2, 3.
[3] Athenagoras, Plea, c. 1, 2.

heathen true notions concerning Christianity. The *earliest* of them lived when persecution was just beginning. Quadratus and Aristides presented apologies to the Emperor Hadrian about the year 120 A.D. Neither of these books is now extant; but Eusebius tells us concerning Aristides,[1] that he was a man faithfully devoted to the religion we profess, and that his work had been preserved by many up to his days. And with respect to Quadratus, he says that he wrote because certain malicious persons attempted to harass our brethren, and that his work, still existing, gave evident proofs of the understanding and the apostolic faith of the writer. Quadratus was able to appeal to the testimony of those who had seen the men on whom Christ's healing power had been exerted. Some of these had lived even to his times.

The *last* Defender was Lactantius. He outlived the times of persecution, and wrote an account of the deaths of the last persecutors. He was tutor to the son of the first Christian emperor, and from his eloquence he was honoured with the title of the Christian Cicero.[2]

The Defenders of the Faith in the 2nd century were philosophers, and wrote in Greek. The Defenders of the Faith in the 3rd century were Africans by country, lawyers or rhetoricians by profession, and wrote in Latin.

Some of the Defences were intended to advocate the Christian cause before emperors and rulers of

---

[1] Eus. Hist. Eccl. iv. 3.   [2] Jerome ad Paul. Ep. xlix.

the provinces. Thus Quadratus and Aristides addressed Hadrian; Justin Martyr—Antoninus Pius; Athenagoras, Melito, and Apollinaris—Marcus Aurelius; Tertullian and Cyprian—African governors. Others were addressed to private persons or the public generally. Thus Theophilus of Antioch wrote three letters to Autolycus, a heathen. Tatian addressed the Greeks; Tertullian and Arnobius, the nations; Justin Martyr, the Jews. More commonly the Defence is made against popular clamour and to remove all pretexts for persecutions; but one book, the "Defence of Origen," is a reply to a book called "The True Word," an attack on Christianity written by the philosopher Celsus.

When we come to inquire what results these books produced, we find very slight material for forming an opinion. Antoninus Pius is said to have put a stop to persecution after reading Justin's Apology, but the story is of doubtful truth.[1] Like most other Christian work, the work done by the Defenders of the Faith is hidden from the eyes of men. Still, it must not be denied, that books had not the great influence then they have now. Every single copy had to be made by hand.[2] Some of the greatest works only existed in one copy. But this we may say with confidence, whatever good the works of the Apologists did the Christian cause in their day, they will certainly do us great good in our day. They give us such a

---

[1] Eus. Hist. Eccl. iv. 12, 13.
[2] Still, slave labour was plentiful and cheap. Cf. 'Church Quarterly Review,' MSS. and Miniatures, vol. v. p. 451.

wonderful picture of Christian life and the Christian society in those early times; and they convince us of the mighty works which may be wrought by those who with all their heart and soul trust in Christ the Lord.

The Defenders of the Faith give us a picture of the darkness which covered the earth, and the gross darkness which covered the peoples, before the true Light came into the world. Then they picture to us Light and Darkness struggling together, and little by little the Light conquering, and shining more and more unto the perfect day. We need the testimony of those who, with enlightened eyes, saw the darkness before the dawn, to tell us how great that darkness was. It was a shame even to speak of those things which were done of the heathen, not only in secret but in public, not only in their games and shows, but also at their most solemn religious festivals, and in the temples of their gods. The Defenders of the Faith tell us of this, and they tell us, too, how Christianity came into a dark and corrupt world and brought with it new light and life. Old bonds were being dissolved, but Christianity established a new brotherhood, of whose members it was said that they loved one another even before they knew one another.[1] Men were enslaved by their lusts and passions, but those whom Christ set free were free indeed. The world was without hope beyond the grave; Christians despised death in the certainty of a happy resurrection.

[1] Octavius, c. 9.

Thus the Defenders of the Faith tell us what a power Christianity has, and wherein that power consists. We, in our day, as we know, have the same source of strength that they had. When we read what they did, we rise comforted with the thought that Christ's grace is sufficient for us also. If the Roman Empire could not destroy the Church in its infancy, no action of the State can destroy the Church in its mature strength.

And now let us consider our subject more particularly in four chapters. The Christians were attacked, and the Apologists defended them; so the first chapter will be The Defence. As we learn from military tactics, no army can be successful which stands only on the defensive, and the Christians, we know, had to wage an aggressive war; so the Apologists in their turn made an attack on the heathen religion and philosophy; hence the second chapter will be The Attack. Besides this, the Apologists give us, by the way, much interesting information concerning themselves and their religion; so the third chapter will be Christians and Christianity. Lastly, leaving Apologetic literature as a whole, we shall consider the different Apologies with their Authors separately; so our fourth and fifth chapters will be The Latin and Greek Apologists and their Apologies.

CHAPTER IV.

THE DEFENCE.

THREE kinds of charges were brought against the Christians by the heathen—Moral, Theological, and Political. It was said they lived immoral lives; that they had no religion, or a bad one, or at least an illegal one; that they were traitors to the Emperor, and enemies of the public good. The first two excited the popular hatred, and were the causes of the tumultuous risings; the last furnished the subject-matter of the legal charge when they were brought before the courts.

The charge of Immorality seems, at first, to have been the most prominent: it sprung, no doubt, from the suspicious jealousy with which the secret meetings of the Christians were viewed. The persecutions rendered it necessary that the Christian worship should be conducted in secret and by night. Before the light, as Pliny tells us,[1] the Christians met together in prayer to Christ. The heathen husband, whilst it was yet dark, missed his wife from his side, and vaguely suspected evil.[2] Arguing from the heathen rites, it was thought that the Christian mysteries must be impure. Rumour soon gave shape to vague sus-

---

[1] Pliny's letter to Trajan.   [2] Tert. ad Uxorem, ii. 4.

picion. "About the modest supper-room of the Christians," says Tertullian, "a great ado is made."[1]

The ceremony of initiation into the society, it was said, was an abominable crime.[2] The neophyte was caused to stab unawares an infant to death, and then all, in greedy haste, tore it limb from limb and devoured it. The feasting was carried to excess. At a given signal the light was put out and all indulged in promiscuous lust. Origen tells us the Jews were the authors of these charges[3]—a thing likely enough in itself; but whether this was so or not, it is easy to see the foundation in fact for the calumny. The heathen had heard of the Eucharistic food of the Body and Blood of Christ, and of the love-feasts. To the first they would be incapable of giving a spiritual significance; the second had but one meaning to an impure imagination; love and lust were, alas! to the heathen of the day, almost interchangeable terms. Religious ceremonies and gross immoralities were closely connected in his experience. Purity was so rare that he disbelieved in its existence. Outward self-restraint was, in his idea, only a cloak to secret immorality: hence he distorted the love-feasts into licentious orgies, and the feeding on the Body and Blood of Christ into murdering and devouring an infant.

For these charges,[4] Tertullian assures us, the heathen had lying rumour as their only witness: and yet the secret of the Christian meetings was by no means well kept. He says,[5] "We are daily beset

---
[1] Tert. Apol. c. 39. [2] Octavius, c. 9.
[3] Orig. c. Celsum, vi. 27; see also Just. Dial. c. 17.
[4] Tert. Apol. c. 7. [5] Ib.

by foes, we are daily betrayed; we are ofttimes surprised in our meetings and congregations. And yet," he asks, "who has ever happened on an infant wailing? Who has found any trace of uncleanness in his wife? Where is the man who, when he had discovered such atrocities, concealed them, or, whilst dragging the guilty before the judge, was bribed to silence?" As a matter of fact, the authorities from time to time did their best to procure evidence, and failed.[1] Pliny investigated the nature of the Christian society in a thorough manner. He had no liking for it, quite the reverse; it was, in his eyes, "an absurd and immoderate superstition." The Christians were possessed with "infatuation"; they were filled with "a contumacious and inflexible obstinacy." But this is the worst he has to say. He searched, but could not find any basis for a criminal charge. He questioned apostates, and they were quite willing, for their own safety, to revile the name of Christ; but even they did not venture to blacken the fair fame of the Christians. Their evidence went no further than this, that the Christians were wont to assemble together before day, for prayer to Christ; for binding all together, by a solemn sacrament, to abstain from all kinds of sin; and for eating a harmless meal. Two deaconesses fell into Pliny's hands, and he put them to the torture, but he could get nothing out of them to his purpose. The conclusion he comes to is this: the Christians are superstitious, they are obstinate, they will not obey the laws, but they are not criminal. In

---

[1] Justin (Apol. ii. c. 12) says that some female slaves were forced by torture to confess the charge.

fact, Pliny's report to Trajan might be summed up in the words, " I can find no occasion against these men, except I find it against them concerning the law of their God."

Pliny's investigation was made at the beginning of the second century, in Bithynia. About fifty years afterwards a violent persecution broke out in Gaul. Reports of the vile doings of the Christians had been circulated amongst the common people until they were goaded to madness. Vettius Epagathus, a young man of blameless life, was refused a hearing when he undertook to show, on behalf of his brethren, that nothing impious was done amongst them. Was he a Christian? the governor asked. He was. That was sufficient; his mouth was stopped, and he was numbered amongst the martyrs.[1]

The heathen slaves of Christian martyrs were apprehended; they saw their masters suffering, and, in fear for themselves, falsely accused them of unnatural crimes. Then, as our account runs, "When the rumour of these accusations was spread abroad, all raged against us like wild beasts; so that if any formerly were temperate in their conduct to us on account of relationship, they then became exceedingly indignant and exasperated against us. And thus was fulfilled that which was spoken by our Lord: " The time shall come when every one who slayeth you shall think that he offereth service to God."[2]

The threat of torture had been sufficient to cause the heathen slaves to accuse their masters. Its ap-

[1] Eus. Eccl. Hist. v. 1.   [2] Ib.

plication was not sufficient to extort a confession from the Christians themselves; and yet, we are told, they suffered pains beyond description, Satan striving eagerly that some of the evil reports might be acknowledged by them.

Sanctus, a deacon, nobly endured all the sufferings that man could devise, and had but one word on his lips, "I am a Christian." His body, with wounds, lost human shape, but in him Christ wrought great wonders; showing to the rest that there is nothing fearful where there is the Father's love, and nothing painful where there is Christ's glory.

For Blandina, a weak slave, all—even her Christian mistress—feared; but she baffled her tormentors though they did their worst, and in the midst of all her sufferings she found strength, and refreshment, and insensibility to pain, in saying, "I am a Christian, and there is no evil done amongst us."

One more faithful witness—the most faithful of all. All had not stood firm; some had by their conduct caused evil reports and were sons of perdition, but others were won back again by the martyrs' prayers. One of these latter was Biblias. "The devil," such is the account, "thinking he had already swallowed her, and wishing to damn her still more by making her accuse (the brethren) falsely, brought her forth to punishment, and employed force to constrain her, already feeble and spiritless, to utter accusations of atheism against us. But she, in the midst of the tortures, came again to a sound state of mind, and awoke, as it were, out of a deep sleep, for the temporary punishment reminded her of the eternal punishment in hell; and she contradicted the accusers of Christians, saying, 'How can children be eaten by those who do not think it lawful to partake even of the blood of brute beasts?' And after this she confessed herself a Christian, and was added to the number of martyrs."

And so the devil's craft, as we see, betrayed him; and Christ rescued from his jaws one that was ready to go down into the pit; and the Christians gained a testimony not to be gainsayed. The deacon's testimony was strong, the slave's still stronger, but the testimony of her who had fallen was strongest of all. What could have raised the fallen one but the power of Christ working in her mightily? The witness extorted by suffering must have been for once the witness of truth.

It is interesting to learn that God honoured His martyrs in the eyes of men. Those who stood firm suffered as Christians, and were not ashamed. Those who apostatized suffered as murderers and profligates, and were tormented by their guilty conscience. The one came forth to their execution like "brides going to their bridal"; the others were downcast, and humbled, and weighed down with every kind of disgrace.

The Apologists pointed to such scenes as these, and asked, Is it possible that men who die as you *see* they do, can live as you *say* they do?[1] In truth, the deaths of the Christians were a convincing testimony to the purity of their Christian lives. A life of self-indulgence is not a preparation for a martyr's

---

[1] Tert. Apol. c. 50; Justin Martyr, ii. 12.

death. But those who were ever crucifying the flesh with its affections and lusts after a spiritual manner, were the men likely in the moment of trial to endure bravely the most dreadful suffering. One of the Apologists, Justin Martyr, saw the force of this argument, whilst still a heathen. He tells us,[1] that when he "was delighting in the doctrines of Plato, and heard the Christians slandered, and saw them fearless of death and of all other things which are counted to be fearful, he perceived it was impossible that they could be living in wickedness and pleasure. For what sensual or intemperate man, or who that counts it good to feast on human flesh, could welcome death, that he might be deprived of his enjoyments, and would not rather continue always the present life?"

The Apologists appeal not only to Christian deaths but to Christian lives in defending themselves against this charge.[2] They were able to point to the change which Christianity had effected in the lives of many. Tertullian says that the remarks used to be made, "What a woman she was! how wanton, how gay! What a youth he was! how profligate, how lustful! They have become Christians! So the hated name is given to a reformation of character."[3] And then he tells us further, that the heathen hated Christianity more than they loved goodness. The chaste Christian wife, and the obedient Christian son, and the faithful Christian servant, fared worse after their reformation than beforetime in their wickedness.

[1] Just. Apol. ii. 12.
[2] Orig. c. Celsum, i. 9; Just. Apol. i. 14, ii. 2.
[3] Apol. c. 3.

The prisons were often full of Christians, but their Christianity was their only crime. Christian names were not to be found in the list of criminals. "It is always," the same writer says in another place,[1] "with *your* folk the prison is teeming, the mines are sighing, the wild beasts are fed; it is from *you* the exhibiters of gladiatorial shows always get their herd of criminals to feed up for the occasion. You find no Christian there, except simply as being such; or if one be there in any other capacity, a Christian he is no longer."

Tertullian shows also[2] *how* it is the Christians were so free from crime. Their morality was based on their religion; their moral sense had been educated by a Divine Teacher; their moral code had been taught them by Divine lips; and they expected to be judged by a Divine Judge. Eternal punishment, they believed, was due for sin; eternal life was the reward of goodness. Moreover, the commandment which had been laid upon them was exceeding wide; it reached even to the words of the lips and the thoughts of the heart. So far from injuring another, they patiently suffered injury themselves; so far from killing another, they were forbidden even to be angry. A Christian could not, like a philosopher, teach one thing and do another. He could not promulgate a code of morals, and not live up to it. Unless he were a Christian in deed, he ceased forthwith to be a Christian in name.

Perhaps this charge could hardly have been so

widely believed without some basis of truth, and there is good reason for thinking that some of the heretics brought discredit on the Christian name. The Gnostics taught that matter, *i.e.* the stuff of which the world generally, and so the human body, was composed, was the principle of evil; and the question with them was, how to keep their higher nature uncorrupted by contact with it. One of their two theories was, "Do absolutely as you please; follow your own impulses; don't give the subject a thought, it is not worth the trouble. Nothing your body can do can have any influence upon your spirit." With such a theory we are prepared to hear that the Gnostics led a licentious life. Irenæus tells us,[1] "that they had been sent by Satan to bring dishonour upon the Church; so that men hearing what they say, may turn away from the preaching of the truth; and seeing what they practise, may speak evil of us all, who in fact have no fellowship with them, either in doctrine, or in morals, or in daily life." Eusebius[2] distinctly traces the "impious and absurd suspicions" against the Christians to the Gnostic theory and practice. They taught, he tells us, "that the basest deeds should be perpetrated by those that would arrive at perfection in the mysteries"; and the consequence was, "to the unbelieving Gentiles they offered scope to slander the truth of God, as the report proceeding from them extended with its infamy to the whole body of Christians."

The Gnostic heresy, though in the 2nd century it

had spread far and wide, was not of long duration. With it were extinguished, Eusebius[1] tells us, all the aspersions on our religion. When he wrote,[2] the old calumnies were dropped by all. Still, under Maximin, only a little before, the old charges were revived.[3] In Damascus some harlots were forced by the governor into making a declaration that they had once been Christians, and had been witnesses of their wickedness. These confessions were engraved on brazen tablets, and were published all over the empire. Besides this, acts of Pilate, full of blasphemy against Christ, were forged;[4] and then, by an imperial edict, all schoolmasters were provided with copies, and it was expressly enjoined that every boy should learn the lies by heart. Just then, "the devil had great wrath, knowing that he had but a short time." Within a year the devil was chained.

When persecutors were reduced for evidence to such straits as we have described, it is plain how little occasion had been given to the adversary to speak reproachfully. Indeed, it may be fairly said, that at no time was this charge believed in by intelligent heathens.[5] Certainly it was not believed in by the emperors Trajan and Marcus Aurelius, as their edicts published after inquiry show.[6] The common people believed in it, no doubt; rumour and garbled quotations were sufficient for them, and very likely their

---

[1] Eus. Hist. Eccl. iv. 7.   [2] 330 A.D. *circa*.
[3] Eus. Hist. Eccl. ix. 5.   [4] Ib. ix. 7.
[5] Justin, in his Dialogue with Trypho (c. x.), puts into the mouth of his Jew a confession that the charges were false.
[6] Eus. Hist. Eccl. iii. 33; v. 1.

belief was encouraged by the authorities as useful. But Roman governors knew,—aye, and acted on their knowledge, that there was one thing more terrible to a Christian woman than death itself.[1] In the Diocletian persecution it was common to send Christian virgins to the houses of shame. The persecutors knew that a taint on Christian purity was more terrible than any punishment or any death. Surely enough has now been said on this subject; it would be well indeed if Christ's Church could refute all the accusations made against her members as triumphantly as this.

We pass on to the second charge made against the Christians—the religious one. It was said that they were either worshippers of monstrous things, or that they were atheists and had no God at all. Here, too, the imagination of the heathen seems to have been their chief witness.

A common theory was that they worshipped the head of an ass. Tacitus, according to Tertullian,[2] was the first to put the notion into people's minds. He records a tradition that the Jews in their "exodus" were saved from perishing from thirst by wild asses, and that in their gratitude they consecrated a head of that animal to be their god. Arguing from the connection of Judaism and Christianity, the heathen supposed the Christians worshipped an ass's head also. A little before Tertullian's time, an apostate Jew, a man who hired himself out to fight with wild beasts, carried about through the streets of Rome a caricature of the God of the Christians.¹ He was depicted as having the ears of an ass, hoofed in one foot, carrying a book, and wearing a toga. And the crowd, we are told, believed the infamous Jew.

Others said they worshipped the Sun.² Perhaps there were two reasons for this charge. Sunday was the chief day of worship for the Christians, and they turned to the east whilst they said their prayers.

Others were convinced that they worshipped the Cross.³ Possibly the reason for this was, that the Christians were seen constantly to sign themselves with this sign.⁴

The Emperor Hadrian confounded them with the worshippers of the Egyptian god Serapis.⁵ To him, in his attachment to the old Roman and Greek religions, all foreign religions were alike.

The martyrs' bodies, rescued at such risk, and buried with such care, were thought by some to be the objects of their worship. Polycarp's body was burnt lest they should abandon "The Crucified" and worship him.⁶ For the same reasons the bodies of some slaves martyred during the Diocletian persecution were cast into the sea.⁷

The Apologists, in dealing with these charges, often wax sarcastic.⁸ Pretty fellows you heathens are, to make any objection to our objects of worship! Were

---

[1] Ad Nationes, i. 14.
[2] Tert. Apol. c. 16.   [3] Ib.   [4] Tert. de Coronâ, § 3
[5] See Neander, Church Hist. i. 141, 142.
[6] Eus. Hist. Eccl. iv. 15.   [7] Ib. viii. 6.
[8] Tert. Apol. c. 16 ; Ad Nat. i. 11.

all you say of us true, we should be much better than you. Why should you object to our worship of an ass's head? You have gods with the heads of dogs and lions, and the horns of bucks and rams, and the loins of goats, and the legs of serpents, and wings sprouting from the back or foot. You say we are devoted to asses; but you must confess that you are worshippers of cattle of all kinds. You say we worship the Sun; many of you worship all the heavenly bodies and the clouds.[1] You say we worship the Cross; you undoubtedly worship your military standards.[2]

It may have been injudicious to retort thus sharply whilst making a plea for permission to exist; but, policy apart, the reply is effective enough.

Probably the charge of atheism was more popular and more seriously believed in than any of the above. Men so well hated as the Christians, were sure to be attacked by scandalous reports not half-believed. But the charge of atheism seemed to rest on a good foundation; for the Christians had, or seemed to have, none of those accessories of worship used by all other religions. Certainly the charge made the common people hate them more intensely.

The position of the common people with respect to their religion was in some points very similar to the position of many people now. When all went well they did not trouble themselves much about it; but when misfortune came they were filled with guilty fears. In prosperous times they were wont to offer in sacrifice worn out, scabbed, and corrupting animals;

or they would cut off the head and the hoofs—the portion assigned to the slaves and dogs—and offer them upon the altars.[1] Tragic and comic writers did not shrink from setting forth the gods as the origin of all family calamities and sins. Men had no objection to making merry over the story of their weaknesses and crimes;[2] dramatic literature pictured their vileness; and when their majesty was thus insulted and their deity dishonoured, the world applauded. Even the sanctity of the temples was not respected, they were convenient places for the most licentious deeds.[3] But when disasters came—as in the second century they constantly did—then superstitious fear filled the hearts of all.[4] It was said at once, the gods are angry because their temples have been deserted and their rites neglected.[5] At such times the Christians were a convenient scapegoat.[5] Public religious ceremonies, rain-sacrifices, barefoot processions, were enjoined; and in these the Christians would take no part. Then there were popular risings, all forms of law were set at nought, and this to such an extent that the authorities had to interfere. Tertullian tells us that the heathen thought the Christians the cause of every public disaster and affliction. If, he says, the Tiber rises as high as the city walls, if the Nile does not send its waters over the fields, if the heavens give no rain, if there is an earthquake, if there is a famine or pestilence, straightway the cry is, "Away with the Christians to the lion." It was Nero who set the

---

[1] Tert. Apol. c. 14.
[2] Arnobius, iv. 33-36.
[3] Tert. Apol. c. 15.
[4] Arn. i. 24.
[5] Tert. Apol. c. 40.

fashion of ascribing calamities to the Christians; and his example in this respect was constantly followed in later times. The martyrdom of Ignatius, Bishop of Antioch, seems to have followed on a destructive earthquake. The persecutions under Antoninus Pius, Marcus Aurelius, and Diocletian, followed after various public calamities—pestilences, inundations, earthquakes, and fires. Maximin boasted that his persecution of the Christians had brought back again to the world long-lost abundance, peace, and health.[1] So prevalent indeed was the idea that the Christians were the guilty causes of the calamities of the times, that many of the Apologists set themselves to show that there was no real connection between them. For the most part the Apologists deal with this matter by pointing out that national disasters occurred long before Christians were known, and that the times are not so bad after all.[2] Seasons of scarcity are relieved by times of plenty, disasters in war are compensated for by victories and successes.

"It is three hundred years," says Arnobius,[3] "since we Christians began to exist. Have wars been incessant? Have the crops always failed? Has there never been peace and plenty on the earth? On the contrary, there have often been the most plentiful yields of grain and seasons of cheapness. Victories innumerable have been gained. The boundaries of the Empire have been extended. It would be quite as fair to attribute your prosperity as your calamity to us. Moreover, is it seemly to ascribe anger and

---

[1] Eus. Hist. Eccl. ix. 7.   [2] Arn. adv. Gentes, i. 3–5.
[3] Arn. adv. Gentes, i. 15.

spite to the immortal gods? Do such passions dwell in heavenly minds? Again, if we are the offenders, do the gods need your strenuous advocacy to avenge the insults offered them? By heat and by cold, by tempest and by disease, they can consume us and drive us from the earth; why do they not put forth their power if they are really angry? Moreover, if we alone are the offenders, why does not the punishment fall on us alone? To you let them give good health, to us the worst. On your farms let them send seasonable showers, on ours let them drive away all gentle rain. Let your sheep multiply, and ours be barren. Let your oliveyards and vineyards give their full increase, let ours give not even a single fruit. Let them make the fruits of the earth nutritious to you, but to us let the honey be bitter, the oil rancid, and the wine vinegar. Such is not the case now. To us who are impious no less share in the bounties of life accrues than to you who are pious. On you as well as on us misfortune falls."

Tertullian points out that many calamities befell the world before the coming of Christ. Islands were swallowed up by earthquakes, the world was destroyed by a flood, Sodom and Gomorrha, Vulsinii and Pompeii were destroyed by fire, the Romans were defeated at Cannæ, and their Capitol was besieged, long before the mention of the Christian name. Indeed, as a matter of fact, the Christians lighten the calamities which come upon the earth. When the heathen, with their sacrifices and processions in the times of their calamity and anxiety, are supplicating the gods for deliverance, the Christians, by fasting and prayer, by abstinence from sin and even ordinary enjoyments, assail heaven with their importunities. They touch God's heart, and He is merciful; but Jupiter gets the honour.[1]

Cyprian, in replying to Demetrian, the proconsul of Africa, on this matter, has quite another theory.[2] He confesses that in winter there is not such an abundance of showers, nor in summer so much sun to ripen the corn, that marble is dug in less quantity from the mountains, and that the gold and silver mines show signs of early exhaustion, that strength, skill, and innocence are all failing; and the reason is, the world is growing old.

The Apologists are very careful to free the Christians from the charge of impiety and atheism. Though they do not worship the gods of the heathen, they do serve and worship God.

"To adore," asks Arnobius,[3] "God as the highest existence, as the Lord of all things that be, as occupying the highest place among all exalted ones, to pray to Him with submission in our distresses, to cling to Him with all our senses (so to speak), to love Him, to look up to Him in faith—is this an execrable and unhallowed religion, full of impiety and sacrilege, polluting by its novel superstition ancient ceremonies? Is this the daring and heinous iniquity on account of which the mighty powers of Heaven whet against us the stings of passionate indignation; on account of which you yourselves, whenever the savage desire has seized you, spoil us of our goods, drive us from our

---

[1] Tert. Apol. c. 40.   [2] Ad Demet. c. iii.   [3] Arn. i. 25.

ancestral homes, inflict upon us capital punishment, torture, mangle, burn us, expose us to wild beasts, and give us to be torn by monsters? Does he deserve the name of man who makes such a charge? Can he be reckoned amongst the gods who charges with impiety those who serve the King supreme, or is racked with envy because *His* Majesty and worship are preferred to his own?"

Of course it is very easy to see how the charge of atheism arose. The Christians had no temples and no images, they would take no part in any of the ceremonies of the State religion. Their whole life showed that they despised and loathed heathenism.

Celsus says,[1] "The Christians cannot so much as endure the sight of the temples, altars, and statues." The Christians have no temples, therefore they have no gods, was a convincing argument to a heathen. His religion was purely an external one. It concerned his nation, it concerned his family, it affected his public and domestic life, but it did not purify his desires, and it did not influence his heart. Disbelief in a god was no reason for not sacrificing to him; if the object of desire was criminal, that again was no reason for omitting to ask a god's help. All alike were content to make utility the foundation of religion. Philosophers and statesmen said, with more or less certainty, The religion of the gods is false; but they felt the masses could be hardly controlled without it. The Roman people generally said, By venerating the gods Rome has reached its present height of prosperity.[2]

[1] Orig. c. Celsum, vii. 62.   [2] Tert. Apol. c. 25.

From neglect of the auguries experience tells us disaster has often come. The Christians, who despise the gods, are enemies to the State.[1]

The third charge brought against the Christians, and, in some respect, that of the most importance, was of a political nature. They formed, it was said, a secret society, they belonged to an unlawful and new religion, they were disloyal to the Emperor, and unprofitable to the State.

The jealousy of the Romans against secret societies was very great. The Emperor Trajan went so far as to forbid the formation of a company of firemen at Alexandria. There was necessarily much secrecy about the Christians and their religion, and there was besides much about them to excite suspicion. They were a body of men of all nations growing and spreading every day. They were united by some tie for some unknown purpose; this purpose was plainly of the greatest importance, for everything reckoned valuable by others was neglected by them; the world's honours and the world's pleasures they alike despised. Vague reports of a kingdom which they were setting up were continually floating about, and that was quite enough to excite jealousy in the mind of any Roman governor. Every now and then glimpses of their aims would be seen, and these were nothing more or less than the subversion of the State religion. The Christians, then, belonged to a secret society, and one, apparently, of a dangerous character. But this was not all, Christianity was an "unlawful" religion—a

[1] Octavius of Min. Felix, c. 7.

" new " religion. Now, at first sight it might be thought that one more or one less religion would not have been considered a matter of much importance. The heathen religions were more numerous than the Christian sects now. The heathen had gods many and lords many, and fresh ones were springing up every day. The Roman government was tolerant of all religions. It never called together all peoples, nations, and languages, to worship the golden image which it had set up. No one was persecuted for his opinions; it was quite an understood thing that different nations had different gods. A religion was, as it were, a national characteristic. Just as one nation differed from another in colour, language, customs, and laws, so it differed also in the gods which it worshipped. So it came to pass that the Romans, when they conquered a nation, and incorporated it into their Empire, incorporated also its gods into their Pantheon. Rome, the Mistress of the world, Alexandria, the meeting-place of the world, were the homes of all religions; temples to the different gods stood side by side. The gods and the nations were supposed to be suited the one to the other; the gods took care of the nations, and the nations worshipped the gods. Everybody worshipped the gods of his fathers after the rites of his fathers, and the Government was not careful to inquire what those rites were. Gallio represents the indifference of the Roman State when he said, " If it be a question of words and names, and of your law, look ye to it; for I will be no judge of such matters."[1]

[1] Acts xviii. 15.

But religions being, according to the Roman idea, national characteristics, they could not be changed any more than you could change your nation. Proselytizing was a thing strictly forbidden, it overthrew the object of religions altogether. By the aid of religion, order was much more easily kept; that, indeed, according to some, was its chief use. A superstitious fear, a Roman historian says, was the mainstay of the Roman State.[1] But proselytizing implied controversy, and angry passions, and tumults, and disorder, and all for a mere nothing. One god was, to all intents and purposes, as good as another; and the gods of a nation had a claim on the worship and veneration of the members of that nation.[2]

Now, of course, Christianity could not reap the benefit of such toleration as this. It proclaimed with a loud voice that there was but one God for all nations. In its very essence it was aggressive; the work of its ministers was to go out into the highways and hedges, and compel men to come in. It set itself to the ridiculous (as it seemed) task of bringing all the inhabitants of Asia, Europe, and Libya, Greeks and barbarians, those dwelling in the uttermost ends of the earth, under one law.[3] It interfered with the worship of the national gods, and moreover, it repudiated that worship of the Emperor by which the Romans thought they could unite the world in one religious bond. Very soon we find the Christians overpassing the bounds of Roman tolerance. They were found to be disturbers of the public peace. They would not leave

---

[1] Polybius, vi. 56.   [2] Orig. c. Celsum, v. 25, 35.
[3] Ib. viii. 72.

other people alone, and therefore they were not left alone. The history of the Church in the New Testament shows us this. To avoid a tumult Pilate ordered Jesus to be crucified. Paul is scourged at Philippi as an exceeding troubler of the city. At Thessalonica he is described as a man who has turned the world upside down. He excites disturbance wherever he goes, and is ultimately sent to Rome because of an uproar at Jerusalem. Perhaps it was tumultuous gatherings arising out of Christian controversies which caused the Jews to be expelled from Rome in the reign of Claudius.[1] It is evident that on the Christians would be laid the blame of all such tumults. From a political point of view they were justly blamable. The view of the Roman authorities could be none other than this. This man's teaching attacked people's prejudices; being what it was, it could hardly fail to make them angry, and excite disturbance. We must suppress him, and those like him, if we would have peace.

The "novelty" of Christianity was no unimportant item in the charge against it. "This new religion," Lucian calls it scoffingly.[2] "Why has this new kind of practice entered so late into the world?" was the question of Diognetus.[3] "Your doctrine has but recently come to light," was the common taunt.[4] To bring back the observance of the ancient institutions, ancient laws and discipline, and the worship of the

[1] Cf. Suetonius: Judæos impulsore Chresto assidue tumultuantes Româ expulit.
[2] De Morte Peregrini.   [3] Ad Diognetum, c. 1.
[4] Theoph. ad Aut. iii. 4.

ancestral religion, was the aim of the very last persecution. "The ancient religion ought not to be censured by a new," is a statement in one of Diocletian's edicts.[1] "It is the greatest of crimes to overturn what has been once established by our ancestors, and what has supremacy in the State"; "It is an act of impiety to get rid of the institutions established from the beginning in the various places," says the philosopher Celsus.[2] It was not difficult to answer the objection based upon the novelty of Christianity. Arnobius points out the improvements in science, art, and civilization, and asks whether they are any the worse for being new.[3] He notices that the Romans are constantly changing their habits and modes of life. Granted that the heathen religion was old, it was only a question of degree. "The belief which we hold is new, some day it will be old; yours is old, but at its rise it was new and unheard of. The credibility of a religion cannot be determined by its age, but by its nature.[4] Four hundred years ago our *religion* did not exist, we admit. But two thousand years ago your *gods* even did not exist.[5] Does the Almighty and Supreme God seem to you something new, and do those who adore and worship Him seem to you to be introducing an unheard-of, unknown, and upstart religion? Is there anything older than He? Can anything be found preceding Him? Is not He alone uncreated, immortal, and everlasting? Our religion is not new in itself, but we have been late in learning the true object of worship.[6] Our reli-

---

[1] Quoted by Neander, C. II. i. 200. [2] Orig. c. Celsum, v. 25.
[3] Arn. ii. 66, 67. [4] Ib. c. 71. [5] Ib. c. 72. [6] Ib. c. 73.

gion, it is true, has only lately sprung up on the earth; and the reason is, He who was sent to declare it to us has but lately appeared.[1] Do you ask why this was? We answer, We do not know. We cannot explain the plans of God. But this we may say; in eternal and unbounded ages nothing whatever can be spoken of as late. Where there is no end and no beginning, nothing is too soon, and nothing too late." [2]

And now we are in a position to state the precise way in which the Christians during the first three centuries became obnoxious to the law. They belonged to a religion, not venerable for age, not allowed by law, and not national. They belonged, moreover, to a religion, which, instead of promoting order, caused dissension and tumult all over the world. Christianity, being what it was, could not be placed on the list of allowed religions; to belong to it was therefore a legal offence. In consequence, a Christian's trial was a very simple thing. He was dragged before the judgment-seat by the mob for his unnatural crimes, or for his atheism. The former charge was very difficult to prove, and as for the latter, the judge was probably himself an atheist by conviction; still it was not politic to let him go, for a tumult was made. The judge, like Pilate, often wished to release him; sometimes he ran all risks, and did release him,[3] but more commonly he let the people have their own way. He condemned in legal fashion a man who was unjustly accused. Not his immorality, or his atheism, but his Christianity was the legal charge on which he was condemned. The law said, "The Christians are not permitted to be." The judge had only to ask, "Are you a Christian?" He had only to obtain the confession, "I am," and then there was no need to inquire further into other matters. The Christians, as such, were liable to torture and death.

"Are you a Christian?" This is a simple question to us, but it is one which has caused many a stout man's heart to quail. "Are you a Christian?" He had but to say, No; he had but to throw a little incense on the fire, he had but to revile the name of Christ; and then at once he would be dismissed unhurt, confirmed in his office if he had one, with his property untouched, and his reputation unsullied. He might have been a Christian in days gone by, the law would forgive him that; he might still be a Christian by conviction, of men's opinions the law took no cognizance; if from henceforward he conformed outwardly to the State religion, that was sufficient, the law asked for nothing more.

And soon, too, the authorities discovered that denial and apostasy gave them more than they even asked. The Roman governor with a sneer on his face, the mob with outspoken jeers, the Christians with heartfelt prayers and pity, marked the pale face and hesitating look of the accused, and one and all knew that if he said, "No, I am not a Christian," a Christian *ipso facto* he was no longer. Open denial and apostasy could only be purged by an open confession. And thus all learnt the fact that a Christian's words and deeds were in closest harmony. A philosopher had no objection to take the test and swear by the gods which he had proved had no existence. A Christian who denied the name of Christ ceased to be a Christian in any sense whatever.

If, then, the prisoner pleaded, " Not guilty," his plea was accepted, and he was released. But if he pleaded "Guilty"; if he said, "I am a Christian," what then? Then the struggle began. Surely it is an almost incredible fact in the history of trials of justice, that the attempt should be made to compel men to confess that they were innocent of the crime laid to their charge. Yet so it was. Torture was applied, not to make the accused confess, but to make him deny.[1] That was the great aim the law always had. The desire was, not to punish men who had been Christians, but to exterminate Christianity. It is Tertullian who brings this strange mode of procedure clearly before us.[2] He pictures a man replying to the question with the words, "I am a Christian." "He tells you what he is," says Tertullian; "you wish to hear from him what he is not. Occupying your place of authority to extort the truth, you do your utmost to get lies from us. 'I am,' he says, 'that which you ask me if I am. Why do you torture me to sin? I confess, and you put me to the rack. What should you do if I denied'? Certainly you give no ready credence to others when they deny; when we deny, you believe at once." Tertullian sees in this a proof that it is the Christian name which is being pursued with enmity. "We are put to the torture if we confess, and we are punished if we persevere, and if we deny, we are acquitted, because all the contention is about a name." He points out that the authorities, treating the Christians thus differently from criminals, recognize the fact that Christians are indeed guiltless of crime.

The accounts of Christian trials which have come down to us, all confirm Tertullian's statement. The question and the answer on such occasions seem to have been nearly always the same. "Are you a Christian?" Pliny asks those brought before him. When they confess, he repeats the question twice, with threats; when they persist, he orders them to be punished. "I am a Christian," says Polycarp (they did not need to ask him). To the invitations, "Swear by the fortune of Cæsar"; "Repent, and say, 'Away with the Atheists'!" "Swear, and I will set thee at liberty"; "Reproach Christ,"—the same simple statement is his only reply. Through the Stadium the proclamation is thrice made, "Polycarp has confessed that he is a Christian." And then the only doubt is, what death he shall die.[1] One question only is asked of Ptolemæus when accused before Urbicius at Alexandria; as must needs be with a true Christian, confession is made, and condemnation at once pronounced. A bystander protests, and asks, "What is the ground of this judgment? Why have you punished this man, not as an adulterer, nor fornicator, nor murderer, nor thief, nor robber, nor convicted of any crime at all, but who has only confessed that he is called by the name of Christ?"

[1] Just. Apol. ii. 2.

The only answer the question gets is, "You also seem to be such an one." It is promptly replied, "Most certainly I am," and he too is led away to death, to be in his turn followed by a third. "Are you a Christian?" is the question of the prefect Rusticus to Justin and his fellow-martyrs. "I am a Christian," each replies in turn, "by the command of God," "by the grace of God," "being freed by Christ." "Do what you will, we are Christians, and do not sacrifice to idols." Immediately sentence is pronounced. What need is there of any further instances? The same is true throughout the period of persecution; and is it not cause for deep thankfulness and for pride, that our brothers, following the Apostolic command, did not suffer as murderers, or thieves, or evildoers, or busybodies in other men's matters; but they suffered as Christians, and were not ashamed, but glorified God on this behalf.[1]

But it was very hard for them to resist to blood, when a word would have set them free. Throughout, it was the great object of the judges to make the Christians say that word. Sometimes threats were used; the confessors were threatened with the flames, or the wild beasts, or the brothel.[2] Sometimes a free pardon was offered to all who renounced their faith, whilst instant death was inflicted on those who still stood firm.[3] Sometimes a man was begged to have respect to his old age,[4] sometimes to have compassion

---

[1] 1 Peter iv. 15, 16.

[2] Martyrdom of Polycarp, c. xi.; Eus. Hist. Eccl. viii. 1, 12; vi. 41; The Passion of St. Theodotus.

[3] Eus. v. 1.   [4] Polycarp, Martyrdom, c. 9.

on his youth.[1] Sometimes friends did their utmost to make them recant.[2] A grey-haired father throws himself at his daughter's feet, and with tears he implores her.[3] " Have pity, my daughter," he says, "on my grey hairs. Have pity on your father, if I am worthy to be called a father by you. If with these hands I have brought you up to this flower of your age, if I have preferred you to all your brothers, do not deliver me up to the scorn of men. Have regard to your brothers, have regard to your mother and to your aunt, have regard to your son, who will not be able to live after you." The procurator says, "Spare the grey hairs of your father, spare the infancy of your boy, offer sacrifice for the well-being of the emperors." She answers, " I will not do so." He asks, " Are you a Christian?" and she replies, " I am." Then there was but a step between her and death. But not all were brave and constant, many were overcome by torture, or over-persuaded by their friends. Specially was this the case in the later persecutions. A time of peace and quiet had its drawbacks, it added those to the Church who in times of persecution were ready to fall away. The number of apostates in the Decian and Diocletian persecutions was very great; and, the persecutions over, the Church found the greatest difficulty in dealing with them when they asked for re-admission to communion. The orthodox teaching was very strict. Some of the heretics said that you might deny Christ with your mouth but still confess

---

[1] Polycarp, Martyr. c. 3.   [2] Eus. Hist. Eccl. vi. 41.
[3] Passions of Perpetua and Felicitas.

Him in your heart.[1] The Church always held that those who formally or virtually apostatized committed sin almost if not quite beyond forgiveness on earth. Years of repentance had in every case to precede restoration to full Christian privileges.

Gallienus, in the year A.D. 259, was the first emperor who recognized Christianity as a legal religion.[2] Up to that time the Christians were always liable to be persecuted. The law was against them, although the Emperor or the governors might be on their side. Gallienus gave to the Christians the free exercise of their religion, and the right of holding property; and thus placed the law on their side. The liberty then first granted was withdrawn by later emperors; it was not till Constantine's time that Christianity was firmly established in its position. Under him it became not only an allowed religion, but the religion of the State.

We pass on now to the next political charge, viz., disloyalty to the Emperor. The Christians had "another king, one Jesus";[3] this was the fact which at first excited the jealousy of the State. But when it discovered, as it soon did, that the Christian kingdom was "celestial and angelic, and to appear at the end of the world," it ceased to trouble itself about the matter.[4]

The foundation for the charge of disloyalty was quite different in later times. The Christians were reckoned to be disloyal to the Emperor because they

---
[1] Eus. Eccl. Hist. vi. 38.
[2] Neander, 'History of the Church, vol. i. 194.
[3] Acts xvii. 7.   [4] Eus. Hist. Ecc. iii. 20.

refused to reverence him as divine, to swear by his genius, and to celebrate his festal days. They would not make a god of him, in fact, and so they were reckoned to be traitors.

The Apologists[1] tell us that the Christians were quite ready to pay all human honours to the Emperor; that they prayed for, served, and honoured the Emperor as pious and loyal subjects should. They point out the fact that no Christians are found amongst the conspirators. Indeed, such a thing is impossible, for their religion forbids them to wish, do, speak, or think evil of any one. The Christians, they say, have a special interest in the prosperity of the Roman empire, for they believe that with its fall violent commotions will come upon the world.[2]

The last political charge is unprofitableness to the State, and perhaps no charge had more real foundation in fact.[3]

When we examine the history and read the literature of the Early Church, we cannot fail being struck with the all-absorbing character of Christianity in those early times. A Christian had the hopes and the promises of his religion, and for the most part he had nothing else to call his own. He looked back on the life of Christ Incarnate. He looked forward to the coming of Christ in power and great glory. Both events were very near to him. Christ had but lately come; Christ was very quickly to come. The cloud had but just received Him out of his sight; the clouds were already gathering to accom-

---

[1] Tert. Apol. c. 32.   [2] Ib. c. 32.
[3] Orig. c. Celsum, viii. 55-68.

pany His return. There was nothing on the earth for him to delight in. He had no hold on its riches or its honours, for he could not reckon even on his life. Any day he might have to give up all for Christ, and any day Christ might come again. The state of the world in which he lived, the rapid approach of the world to come—both these produced in him a remarkable singleness of aim.

Hence arose the charge that the Christians were unprofitable citizens. The later Apologists invariably refer to it. Tertullian denies its truth.[1] " How in all the world," he says, " can that be the case with people who are living among you, eating the same food, wearing the same attire, having the same habits, under the same necessities of existence?" "We sojourn with you in the world, abjuring neither forum, nor shambles, nor booth, nor workshop, nor inn, nor weekly market, nor any other place of commerce. We sail with you, and serve in your armies, and till the ground with you. In like manner we unite with you in your trafficking; even in the various arts we make public property of our works for your benefit." The Christians, he tells us, had their own costly religious ceremonies. They spent much on charity, and defrauded none of their due. They did not pander to the luxury and vice of the age; but that was no loss to the State. They cost the Government nothing as criminals, and they alone reckoned themselves to be responsible for their words and looks as well as their deeds. Such is Tertullian's defence in his Apology. It seems to be

[1] Apol. c. 42.

pretty complete, considering the times and the position of the Christians. Unfortunately, in other places, Tertullian seems to contradict himself. He tells us the Christians have in this world no concern, but to depart out of it as quickly as they may.[1] Lactantius again denies the lawfulness of all pursuit of gain.[2]

With principles like these, there would be few busy, thriving merchants among them, ministering either to the luxuries, or even the wants of the people. For another reason, also, commerce was almost closed to them, for they could not protect themselves when cheated. The forms of the law-courts were idolatrous, so that they could not be used with a clear conscience. It was doubtful whether, under any circumstances, lawsuits could be permitted. "It does not become," says Tertullian, "the son of peace to sue at law."[3] The Christians took no part in politics, they despised and refused all temporal honours and ensigns of magistracy.[4] For conscience sake, as we have seen, they abstained from the public games and the temple worships; they brought no custom to the multitudes who derived their livelihood from one or the other. More than all, some of the Christians had conscientious scruples connected with the lawfulness of the profession of arms. Tertullian says, "There is no agreement between the divine and human sacrament, the standard of Christ and the standard of the devil, the camp of light and the camp of darkness."[5]

[1] Apol. c. 41. [2] Div. Inst. v. 17.
[3] Tert. de Coronâ, c. 11.
[4] Tert. Apol. c. 38; Orig. c. Celsum, viii. 75.
[5] Tert. de Idol. c. 19.

If a soldier become a Christian, he says, he must either quit the service or suffer for God's sake.¹ Many of the Apologists held the same opinion on the incompatibility of the military service with the service of Christ. Origen says,² "None fight better for the king than we do. We form a special army for him, an army of piety, by offering our prayers to God; but we do not fight under him, even if he require it." A soldier's duties often brought him in corrupting contact with heathenism: he had to keep guard over the temples, and take meals in them; he had to protect the heathen gods, and had to carry idolatrous flags and badges; he had to take idolatrous oaths, and to join in idolatrous ceremonies.³ Under the circumstances it was almost impossible for a Christian to be a soldier. Tertullian went even further, and settled the matter on abstract principles. The Lord had taken away the sword; in disarming Peter he unbelted every soldier.⁴

It is impossible to conceive a course of conduct better adapted to enrage the Roman Government than this. They could hardly be expected to tolerate the refusal of such a numerous body of men to serve in the ranks as soldiers and to fulfil their duties as citizens. They naturally asked what would become of the State if all were Christians; if there were none to fill the public offices, to provide for the public necessities, to fight against the public foe.⁵ It is true not all the Christians were thus, by their principles, made

---

¹ De Coronâ, c. 11.   ² C. Celsum, viii. 73.
³ De Idol. c. 19; de Coronâ, c. 11, 12.
⁴ De Idol. c. 19.   ⁵ Origen c. Celsum, viii. 68, 69.

useless in the affairs of the world. Clement's exhortation is, " Practise husbandry if you are a husbandman ; but while you till your fields, know God. Sail the sea, you who are devoted to navigation ; yet call the while on the heavenly pilot. Has knowledge taken hold of you whilst engaged in military service? listen to the commander who orders what is right."[1] But in the rise of a new party, the eccentricities or violent statements of a few extreme members are invariably placed to the credit of the whole. In this case the heathen and social systems were so closely intertwined, that a Christian could not join in many of the pursuits of the day. In those open to him, conscientious difficulties were constantly in his path, and dangers to his property and life were continually threatening. Not wishing to court martyrdom, he took refuge in obscurity ; and thus incurred, with some reason, the charge of neglecting his duty as a man living in the world, and as a citizen in the State.

And now our description of " The Defence " is complete ; we have seen all that the heathen had to say against the Christians, and the reply the Christians were able to make. Happy would it have been for the Christians, if their enemies had never been able to accuse them with so little truth, and if their champions had always been able to reply with such convincing force.

[1] Clem. Alex. Cohort. c. 10.

CHAPTER V.

THE ATTACK.

THE Apologists were contending for toleration; that is a fact we must ever bear in mind. So their proper work was *Defence*, not *Attack*. But it was very difficult to defend themselves without attacking the heathen. Being Christians, their object was to subvert all the religions of the world, and put Christianity in their place. Christianity claimed to be The Religion for the world. Its God was the only true God. All other religions were false; their gods were evil spirits, or mere men, or powers of nature, or senseless wood and stone.

Doubtless it would have been more politic for those who were asking for permission merely to exist, to have abstained from carrying the war into the enemy's country. But the Apologists would not, or could not, do this. Attack they must and would. Thus doing, they showed the heathen the intolerant nature of Christianity. At first, the idea of a universal religion was regarded with contempt.[1] Its accomplishment was considered to be beyond all possibility. Later on, the authorities realized their danger, but it was then too late.[2] The Christians had

---
[1] Origen c. Celsum, viii. 72.
[2] Decian and Diocletian Persecutions.

become too powerful, and the battle was virtually won.

When the Apologists attacked the existing heathen religions, they had, so far as argument was concerned, an easy task. The work had been done for them already by the philosophers. The world had outgrown the gods of its childhood. Men, or, at any rate, men of cultivated intellects, had ceased to deify brute force and strong passion. Philosophy had taught many that God was not a man, or like a man, in His nature and attributes. The heathen mythology had been examined, and its historical character utterly destroyed. The truth of the heathen religion was given up. It could not, it was confessed, be rationally defended. Popular discussion upon it was to be avoided, as inevitably tending to the overthrow of its influence on the people.[1] Its overthrow was to be deprecated for many reasons. It would break the connection with the past. It would cause a revolution in the State. It would deprive the authorities of a most useful engine of government. It was much better to leave things as they were. It was much better to receive the teaching of antiquity, and to adore without inquiry. The maintenance of a false religion could do no harm. The overthrow of the religion of the State must produce the greatest calamities.

These sceptical opinions were not wholly confined to the learned few. They were popularized for the masses by the poets and actors. The poets were allowed to invent unseemly tales concerning the gods. Or rather

---

[1] Lact. Div. Inst. ii. 3.

invention was scarcely necessary; they had only to put in an attractive form the disgraceful legends handed down from antiquity. To a still greater degree, the actors in their representations exposed the gods to popular ridicule. At the public games, in the presence of the Priests, the Flamens, the Augurs, and the Vestal Virgins, the gods, in whose honour all were assembled, were so depicted as to expose them to the contempt and abhorrence of all. "May you have a daughter as wicked as she whom you have described," said a spectator to an actor, after hearing the catalogue of Diana's sins.[1] The gods furnished a mark for the low wit and scurrilous jests of the comedians. And this suited the popular taste.[2] When a good hit was made, the spectators, we are told, shouted and rose up, and the whole pit resounded with the clapping of hands and applause. Arnobius remarks that the gods were the only beings unprotected by the laws of libel.[3] To whisper evil of a king was treason. To degrade a magistrate or insult a senator was a crime severely punished. To defame any one in a satirical poem was, by the laws of the Decemvirs, a punishable offence. Even severe affronts had their assigned penalties. Only the gods were unhonoured, contemptible, and vile. About them, and them alone, any one was at liberty to say what he would.

The Roman policy, and the course of events, had greatly helped to weaken the hold of religion on the minds of men. In ancient times the Romans had had

[1] The story is Plutarch's, quoted by Lecky, 'European Morals,' i. 178.
[2] Arnobius adv. Gentes, iv. 36.   [3] Ib. iv. 34.

a religion which, however defective, had served many useful purposes. It did not, as one has observed, make men saints, but it made them patriots.[1] There are many noble examples of self-devotion in Roman history. At the command of the gods many died, not, indeed, for their religion, but for their country. The old Roman religion promoted simplicity and morality of life. It made men better citizens. It filled them with feelings of submission and reverence to the power above them, and beyond them, in whose hands they were. But in later times all this was changed. Conquered Greece enslaved its conqueror. Greek philosophy and Greek religion were introduced into Rome together. The Greek mythology was incorporated into the Roman religion and corrupted it. When the lives of the gods were so wicked, and the rites in which they were worshipped so impure, it could not fail but that religion and morality were altogether dissevered. At the same time Greek philosophy leavened Roman thought, and made it utterly sceptical. The idea of an overruling providence was lost. "If there are gods," Ennius said, and the people applauded, "they do not concern themselves in the affairs of men." Some of the wisest Romans saw the fearful danger to the State, and sought to avert it.[2] The elder Cato, at the very commencement of the mischief, declared the Greeks to be the parents of every vice, and obtained the dismissal of the Grecian teachers. The mysteries of Bacchus and the Egyptian worship

[1] Lecky, 'European Morals,' i. 177.
[2] Cf. Merivale, 'History of the Romans under the Empire,' ii. 512, 513.

were, in the interest of morality, once and again expelled from Rome by the Senate. But all efforts were in vain. The corruption in morals and faith was too wide-spread. The old Roman religion was too simple and severe to compete with the new, attractive, and sensual worship. And so in the Apologetic period the state of things was this :—There was a religion which would not bear examination, and which taught immorality. It had gods in whom many did not, in any sense, believe; and whom none, whoever they were, could respect. Those who worshipped them did so from a base, and not an ennobling, fear. To them, sacrifice, but not reverence, was due. You might ask them to exercise their power for the vilest objects. If your prayers were unheard, you punished them by overturning their altars and dishonouring their images.[1]

It was evidently not a difficult task for the Apologists to attack such a religion as this; indeed, before their attack was made, the defence on rational grounds had ceased. Nevertheless, though the heathen religion had ceased to have any moral influence on the habits of the people, though it had ceased in any sense to control thought, it still remained a mighty political engine not to be meddled with, and the force of superstition was never more strong.[2] The man who did not believe in the existence of a god, believed in the influence of the stars, and dared not disregard omens. The people who made the gods a laughing-stock in the theatres, believed that life and

---

[1] Cf. Lecky, 'European Morals,' i. 178.   [2] Ib. i. 179.

prosperity were in their power. So the attack, though easy in one respect, was very dangerous in another. You might, if you pleased, like the philosophers, expose the folly of the religion of the gods, but you must not seek to overthrow the religion of the State and the religion of the people.

And now to notice cerain points in the Apologetic attack; and first, the Polytheistic nature of the heathen religion.

The Apologists argue the absurdity of supposing that there can be more than one God existing from everlasting. To suppose there are many is to circumscribe the power of each.[1] Division of Deity destroys the perfection of Deity; what belongs to the one god is wanting to the other; just as there is only room for one ruler in an empire, for one general in an army, and one master in a house, so there is only room for one God in the universe.[2] The bees have one king, the flocks one leader, amongst the herds there is one ruler; so He who has ordered and who governs heaven and earth is One. Even the poets have announced "The *One* Father of gods and men." The philosophers, though differing in the way they express the truth, teach the unity of the Divine Power, and Mind, and Providence.[3] One of them[4] tells us, "The gods of the people are many, but the God of nature is One."

The second objection to the heathen religion is that it is a worship of things earthly and material. Some of the Apologists regard it as mere image-worship.

---

[1] Lact. Div. Inst. i. 3. [2] Octavius, c. 18.
[3] Octavius, c. 19. [4] Antisthenes.

Thus Theophilus, writing to Autolycus, says, he had assailed him with empty words, boasting of his gods of wood and stone, hammered and cast, carved and graven, which neither see nor hear, for they are idols, and so the works of men's hands.[1] So, also, the author of the Epistle to Diognetus, who asks,[2] "Is not one of your gods a stone, similar to that on which we tread? Is not a second brass, in no way superior to ordinary vessels? Is not a third wood, already rotten? Is not a fifth iron, consumed by rust? Is not a sixth earthenware, like the commonest vessel? Did not the sculptor fashion one, the brazier a second, the silversmith a third, and the potter a fourth? Are they not all deaf, blind, without life, destitute of feeling, incapable of motion, liable to rot? Do not ye mock and insult them far more than the Christians, when ye worship those made of stone and earthenware, without appointing any persons to guard them? But those made of silver and gold ye shut up by night, and appoint watchers to look after them by day, lest they be stolen."

Arnobius, especially, is scathing in his sarcasm on this aspect of the heathen religion.[3] Why is it, he asks, "O men, that you, of your own accord, cheat and deceive yourselves by voluntary blindness? These images which fill you with terror, and before whom you prostrate yourselves, were compacted, it may be, of a harlot's gauds or a woman's ornaments, of camels' bones or elephants' teeth, of cooking-pots and little jars, of candlesticks and lamps, or of other less

---

[1] Theoph. ad Aut. i. 1.   [2] Ad Diognetum, c. 2.
[3] Adv. Gentes, vi. 14–16.

cleanly vessels; and having been melted down they were cast into these shapes, and came out the forms which you see, baked in potters' furnaces, produced by anvils and hammers, filed down with files, divided with saws, cleft and hewn with axes, hollowed out by the turning of borers, and smoothed with planes. Is it not incredible folly to believe in, to kneel trembling before, a god which you yourself made with care, which is the product of the labour of your hands? Suppose some one were to place copper, silver, gold, etc., in the lump, or bits of broken statues before you, and were to bid you to slay victims and give divine honours to them, would you obey? You answer, No one is so stupid as to class material substances like these among the gods.[1] What then! Do the fashioning and the working-up of the material, the receiving of the form of a man, give the power of deity and the rank of heavenly beings? Does fashioning, even, change copper into gold, or compel worthless earthenware to become silver? And yet you men, rational beings, sink down before pieces of baked earthenware; you adore plates of copper; you beg, from the teeth of elephants, good health, office, power, gain, good harvests, rich vintages. Would that you could only look at your gods from the inside, you would see that they were kept from falling to pieces by dovetails, and clamps, and brace-irons. You would see that lead is run into their hollows and joints to give them permanence. You would find faces without the back parts of the head, hands

---

[1] Adv. Gentes, vi. 15.

without arms, wood and stone mixed incongruously. But, after all, it is not necessary to look inside. Do you not see those images, whose feet and knees you grasp at prayer, falling into ruins from the dropping of rain, decaying and becoming rotten, blackened by the smoke of the sacrifices, eaten away with rust? Do you not see that newts, shrews, mice, and cockroaches, which shun the light, build their nests and live in the hollow part of these statues? that they gather carefully all kinds of filth and other things suited to their wants, hard and half-gnawed bread, bones laid up for a time of scarcity, rags, down, and paper, to make their nests soft, and keep their young warm? Do you not see sometimes over the face of an image cobwebs and treacherous nets spun by spiders to entrap imprudent flies? Do you not see the swallows flying within the temples, bedaubing the mouths, beard, eyes, noses of the deities with their excrement? Blush, and learn from dumb creatures that there is nothing divine in images, into which they do not fear or scruple to cast unclean things.

"But you say, These images are not themselves the gods, but the gods dwell in them as dedicated to their use. What! do the gods leave heaven to dwell in gypsum and earthenware? Why should they prefer these prisons to their starry seats? Are they obliged to be there, and always there? or have they free passage to go when and where they please? What more wretched beings than they, if hooks and leaden bonds hold them fast on their pedestals? If, on the other hand, they can fly forth when they choose, it follows that the images at these times cease to be gods, and sacrifices should not be then offered to them. Before you sacrifice you ought to inquire whether the gods are at home. Then does each god dwell wholly in one image, or is he divided into parts and members? There are ten thousand images of Vulcan in the world: can he be at one time in all the ten thousand? This is utterly impossible, seeing he has the form of a man. The whole cannot exist without its parts. If, again, the gods dwell in the images, why do you guard, protect, and keep them shut up under the strongest keys, iron bars, and bolts, guarded by a thousand men and a thousand women, lest some thief should by chance enter in? Why do not the gods avenge insults like that which Dionysius committed, when he despoiled Jupiter of his golden vestment and gave him one of wool instead, saying that gold was cold in winter and heavy in summer, whilst wool was fitted for both seasons? Why do they not deliver themselves when their shrines are destroyed by earthquake, and tempest, and fire, or robbed by their own priests from within, or thieves from without?

"The images are neither the deities themselves, nor the habitations of the deities, but merely the representations of the deities, was a third hypothesis. Pretty representations they are, was the reply. The wanton fancy of your artist has given forms to your gods at which even the sternest might laugh; and your celebrated courtezans have been models for your goddesses. Under any circumstances, how do you know your representations are correct? It may happen that in heaven one has a beard, who by you is represented with smooth cheeks; that another is advanced in years, to whom you give the appearance of a youth. At the very best you are giving your gods the forms of men. Have, then, the immortal gods the weaknesses and inconveniences inseparable from the bodies of men?

"What shall we say then?" says Arnobius,[1] "that the gods have a head modelled with perfect symmetry, bound fast by sinews to the back and breast, and that to allow the necessary bending of the neck, it is supported by combinations of vertebræ and by a bony foundation? But if we believe this to be true, it follows that they have ears also, pierced by crooked windings; rolling eyeballs overshadowed by the edges of the eyebrows; a nose, placed as a channel through which waste fluids and a current of air might easily pass; teeth to masticate food, of three kinds, and adapted to three services; hands to do their work, moving easily by means of joints, fingers, and flexible elbows; feet to support their bodies, regulate their steps, and prompt the first motions in walking. But if they bear these things which are seen, it is fitting that they should bear those also which the skin conceals under the framework of the ribs. You say, also, that they have not only bodies but that they have also sex."[2] "What shall we say then? that gods beget and are begotten? Who, however mean his capacity, does not know that the sexes have been ordained by the Creator to renew and maintain that which is fleeting and transient? Are, then, the

---

[1] Adv. Gentes, iii. 12.   Ib. iii. 8,9.

gods mortal? If not, countless heavens will not be able to contain the multitude of their offspring."

"Then again," he asks, "if the gods have bodies, are these bodies marked by a difference in the contour of their forms?[1] If so, some have big heads, prominent brows, broad brows, thick lips; others of them have long chins, moles, and high noses; these have dilated nostrils, these are snub-nosed; some are chubby from a swelling of their jaws or growth of their cheeks; some are dwarfed, others are tall or of middle size; some are lean, others sleek or fat; some have crisped and curled hair, others are shaven or with bald and smooth heads. Your workshops show and point out that our opinions are not false, inasmuch as, when you form and fashion gods, you represent some with long hair, others smooth and bare; as old, as youths, as boys, swarthy, grey-eyed, yellow, half-naked, bare, or, that cold may not annoy them, covered with flowing garments thrown over them." "Is not this really degrading, most impious, and insulting, to attribute to the gods the features of a frail and perishing animal?"

"But you say, perhaps, that you have given the gods the appearance of men merely to do them honour, and that they have, indeed, other forms.[2] Supposing that asses, dogs, and pigs had any human skill in contrivance, and wished to do us honour by some kind of worship, should we not be greatly enraged if they determined that our images should bear and assume the fashion of their own bodies? Why do you then insult the gods in a similar way?"

[1] Adv. Gentes, iii. 14.   [2] Ib. iii. 16.

"Then you ascribe to the gods not only human bodies, but also human offices.[1] You represent them, some as artificers, some physicians, others working in wool, sailors, players on the harp and flute, hunters, shepherds, and, as there was nothing more, rustics. And that god, men say, is a musician; and this other can divine. One is instructed in obstetric arts, another trained up in the science of medicine. Is each, then, powerful in his own department? and can they give no assistance, if their aid is asked, in what belongs to another? Why should the gods be acquainted with these human handicrafts, and arts, and sciences? Are there forests in heaven that Diana may hunt? Are the gods liable to diseases and wounds, so that the assistance of Æsculapius is needed? Do they engage in agriculture or in war, so that they require Vulcan's tools or weapons? Do they need to be covered with garments, so that Minerva has to spin and weave cloth, and make tunics suited to the season of the year? Surely, neither the divine necessities nor the divine nature require any such ingenuity or mechanical skill."

But the history of the gods is the most favourite field for the Apologetic attack. That history showed that the gods had a beginning, that the world was created before them, and that men lived before them. That history showed that to them belonged all the weaknesses of weak men, the unrestrained passions of bad men, and the most heinous crimes of the worst of men. How could they talk of the immortal gods when their sepulchres were with them unto this

[1] Arn. iii. 20.

day? How could they believe the legends when they were not consistent one with another? The theologians spoke of three Joves, and five Junos, and five Mercuries, and five Minervas. Arnobius pictures the five Minervas hovering over their altar, and each claiming for herself the sacrifice offered to the goddess of her name.[1] Following the various traditions, he represents one claiming as mother of Apollo and Diana; the second, as the offspring of the Nile; the third, as the warlike descendant of Saturn; the fourth, as the goddess who sprang from the head of Jove; the fifth, as the virgin who slew her wicked father Pallas. What judge, he asks, is to decide between such great personages? Would it not be better, on the whole, for a man to have nothing to do with any of them, lest, sacrificing to one, and perhaps the wrong one, he should make enemies of the rest? The Apologists attack the heathen mythology with unnecessary minuteness. We cannot follow them here to any profit. The story of the lives of the gods is too corrupting for men to read. Truly not those who denied, but those who invented and believed such stories, were the real blasphemers of the gods.

The untenability of the heathen mythology in its literal meaning had been seen and confessed by their own writers.[2] Some of them said that it was not intended to be history, but allegory. The gods were the powers of nature personified. According to the Stoic explanation, " Neptune was the sea, Pluto was

---

[1] Arn. adv. Gentes, iv. 16.   [2] Ib. iv. 32.

fire, Hercules represented the strength of God, Minerva His wisdom, Ceres His fertilizing energy."[1] According as the power of God was manifested, in heaven or on earth, in the sea or in hell, He had different names given Him. The objection to this theory was that it did not account for the facts. You might thus make a pretty little allegory here and there, but the mass of the stories became nothing but nonsense. Besides, why, it was asked, was it necessary to put pure ideas into an obscene dress?[2] The result was, that what was venerable was vilely spoken of, and the basest deeds were ascribed to the gods.

But, after all, said the Romans, the religion of the gods is true, for it is by worshipping them that Rome has reached its present height of prosperity. You put the cart before the horse, is the Apologetic answer. Rome's prosperity preceded Rome's worship of the gods.[3] The first Romans were "abandoned, profligate, incestuous, assassins, and traitors"; and the Roman State laid its foundations in blood and rapine. Irreligious Romulus preceded pious Numa. The Romans have ever been wont first to conquer a nation, and then to worship its gods. Is it possible, then, that they owe their prosperity to powers which could not defend their own worshippers? They conquered gods and spoiled their temples, before they professed to adore them and conquer by them. The truth is, the Romans are not so great because they are religious, but because they have been sacrilegious with impunity. But, you say, see what disasters have

[1] Lecky, 'European Morals,' i. 171.
[2] Arn. v. 40, 41.   [3] Octavius, c. 26.

resulted from neglecting the auguries. Well, it is quite true, Clodius and Flaminius and Julius would not wait for the greedy pecking of the chickens, and afterwards lost their armies. But what about Regulus? he observed the auguries, and was taken captive. Paulus had greedy chickens at Cannæ, and yet he was utterly overthrown. Caius Cæsar despised the auspices, and conquered all the more easily and quickly. Thus there are facts on both sides.

But what was the secret of the power of the false religions over men? The Apologetic answer is, "The demons or evil spirits."[1] They describe their origin, nature, and method of working. They reckon them to be the offspring of the intercourse of the sons of God with the daughters of men. They are spiritual beings whose great business is the ruin of mankind, body and soul. Unseen and unfelt, their working can only be traced in its effects. They are everywhere in a single moment, the whole world is as one place to them. They are the poison in the breeze which blights the produce of the earth, in bud, and flower, and maturity. They are the taint in the atmosphere which spreads the pestilence. They breathe into the soul and rouse up its latent corruption. They hung upon the lips of the prophets and learned thus the course of future events, and then set up false Christs and false prophets. They inspired the oracles; hence it was the Pythian at Delphi was able to declare so wonderfully what Crœsus was at that moment doing in far-off Lydia; the demon inspiring the oracle

---

[1] Tert. Apol. c. 22, 23; Lact. Div. Inst. ii. 15–18; Just. Apol. i. 54–57, ii. 5.

had gone and returned in a moment. They give disease in order to have the credit of curing it, and all in order that men should believe in the deity of stones, and not seek after the only true God. Powerful as they are, they quail when adjured by Christians in the most sacred Name. " Fearing Christ in God, and God in Christ, they become subject to the servants of God and Christ. So at our touch and breath, overwhelmed by the thought and realization of the judgment fires, they leave at our command the bodies they have entered, unwilling, distressed, and ashamed before your presence." [1]

This connection of the heathen idols with devils was a matter of considerable practical importance to the Christians. The philosophers had no objection to offer sacrifice or burn incense to gods which had no existence. They considered such an act to have no meaning in itself, but to be part of their duty as citizens of the State. It did them no harm, and it did others good. They regarded it as we should regard some of the forms of society or ceremonies of public life. But the Christians, believing the temples to be the dwelling-places, and the sacrifices to be the food, of devils,[2] regarded all participation in the ceremonies of the heathen religion as nothing less than devil-worship. They, unlike the philosophers, owed allegiance to a master, Christ they owned as their Lord.[3] To share, to the slightest degree, in any idolatrous ceremony was to forsake that allegiance, and to join in covenant with that devil whom at their baptism they

[1] Tert. Apol. c. 23, 24. [2] Athenagoras, c. 26.
[3] Lact. Div. Inst. v. 20, 21.

had renounced. They could not, for one moment, take refuge in the plea of the unmeaningness and emptiness of the act. It was to them nothing less than replacing a broken yoke of bondage round their necks. Moreover, why should they worship beings of inferior power to themselves? The weakest Christian, they believed, was by the power of Christ stronger than the strongest devil.[1] Your divinities are subject to us Christians, and we are ready to prove it to you openly any day, is Tertullian's taunt. God has enlightened our eyes, and delusions of devils have no longer power to deceive us, is the assertion of many Apologists.[2] With such a belief a Christian could have no trifling with any idolatrous ceremony lest he should be again taken captive to do the devil's will.

Such are the main points of the Apologetic attack on the heathen religion. As we have seen, very real in its power, very noxious in its influence, that religion seemed. To the light and liberty, love and purity, of the religion of Christ, it presented a most fearful contrast. What wonder is it that the defenders of the faith could not help attacking it in season and out of season? The importance of their attack to us lies in this. From it we learn what the world was before the Christian revelation. We see the gods which men invented for themselves, and we learn to prize more highly the light which we enjoy.

But Christianity had a more dangerous enemy than the religion of the gods, viz. the heathen philosophy.

---

[1] Lact. Div. Inst. iv. 27; Tert. Apol. c. 23.
[2] Just. Apol. i. 5; Athenagoras, c. 27; Tert. Apol. c. 22, 23.

To it, and not to religion, the wisest men turned when seeking a remedy for the corruptions of the age.

Pure and noble as much of the heathen philosophy was, it was not difficult to attack it on the practical side. It had destroyed the heathen religion, but it could put nothing in its place. By its own confession it had done nothing, and could do nothing. It disclaimed pronouncing with certainty on any matter.[1] All human things were dubious. Probabilities, not truths, were the results of its inquiries. After many years of inquiry it deliberated still. It was not given to man to know what is above the earth or under the earth. It was not wise for him to wander beyond his earthly limits. The wisest of men had said, "That which is above us concerns us not."[2] The confession of ignorance is the height of wisdom to which man can attain. The longer the research, the obscurer the truth became.

This was all the wise men of the world could do for it. They could expose error, but they could not discover truth.[3] They searched into the darkness, and they brought back no tidings of a guiding light, they said, The darkness deepens the further we go.[4] The study of philosophy brought with it no joy, but an ever-increasing conviction that man was born to sorrow, and that there was no well-founded hope of a life beyond the grave.[5] "All hope abandon ye who enter here," was the inscription which first met the eye of the student in the Stoic school. The world

---

[1] Octavius, c. 5.   [2] Ib. c. 13.
[3] So Cicero lamented.
[4] Döllinger's 'Jew and Gentile,' ii. 129.   [5] Ib.

and men will be destroyed, because of their wickedness; the new world and new race will soon be just as bad, was Seneca's teaching.[1] "Let us eat and drink, for to-morrow we die," was the true philosophy of life. On the tombs are found such inscriptions as these:[2] "What I have eaten and drunk, that I take with me; what I have left behind me, that have I forfeited." "Reader, enjoy thy life; for after death there is neither laughter nor play, nor any kind of enjoyment." The old heathen stories of the other world were false. "Pilgrim, stay thee, listen and learn. In Hades there is no ferry-boat, nor Charon, the ferryman; no Æacus or Cerberus; once dead, we are all alike."[3] The philosophers could see the whole creation groaning and travailing in pain, but to them the pangs were pangs of death, and not pangs of birth. They were able to discern evil in the world, but they knew of no deliverance. They became doubtful of such a thing as divine justice in life, and incredulous of a retribution after death. They were not certain whether human affairs were set agoing by destiny and immutable necessity, or by hazard.[4] Most, of all things, they needed an example. The Stoics admitted that the ideal man had never yet appeared upon the earth.[5] Cicero describes the rapture with which such an one would be received. There was not amongst them, as amongst the Jews, a well-grounded expectation of "One who should come" to be the Deliverer from evil and the Example of good. The indefinite hope

---

[1] Döllinger's 'Jew and Gentile,' ii. 126.
[2] Quoted by Döllinger, ii. 14.   [3] Ib. p. 139.
[4] Cicero de Repub. vi. 24; Octavius, c. 5.   [5] Döllinger, ii. 129.

of the coming golden age, which was all any heathen had, was to them but a popular superstition.

And, indeed, philosophy in early Christian times, had, like all other things, degenerated.[1] The Apologists constantly describe the vices of its professors.[2] In the case of many, the philosophic garb was their only claim to the name philosopher. Tatian describes them as men who left uncovered one of their shoulders, who let their hair grow long, who cultivated their beards, and who allowed their nails to become like the claws of wild beasts. They said they wanted nothing, and wanted many things. They spoke with an assumption of authority, and revenged themselves if contradicted; they indulged in abuse if they were unpaid, and their philosophy was but the art of getting money. Lactantius[3] gives Seneca's definition of philosophy, viz., "The right method of living, or the art of passing a good life"; and then he goes on to say that of philosophers there has been seldom one who has done anything praiseworthy in his life. "Who is there," he asks, "who does not see those men are not teachers of virtue, who are themselves destitute of virtue? for if any one should diligently inquire into their character, he will find they are passionate, covetous, lustful, arrogant, wanton, and concealing their devices under a show of wisdom, doing those things at home which they had censured in the schools."

This defect in the philosophers was confessed by the heathen. Cicero said[4] there were few who thought

---

[1] Döllinger, ii. 156.   [2] Tatian, Orat. c. 2.
[3] Div. Inst. iii. 15.
[4] Quoted by Lactantius, Div. Inst. iii. 15.

true instruction, not a display of knowledge, but a law of life; few who were obedient to themselves and submitted to their own decrees. Some were so filled with levity and ostentation, that they had better not have learned at all. Some were eagerly desirous of money, others of glory. Many were the slaves of lusts, so that their speech wonderfully disagreed with their life. Cornelius Nepos said, none had greater need of teachers of living than those who discussed a rule of life. Seneca said, that philosophers denouncing avarice, lust, and ambition, seemed to be making a description of themselves. They were like physicians whose advertisements contained medicine, and their medicine-chests poison. Most clever were they at inventing excuses for committing unphilosophic crimes in a philosophic manner. Seneca also said, the philosophers were not ashamed of their vices, but invented defences for their baseness, that they might appear even to sin with honour. They would not abandon good morals, but adapt them to the occasion; all things which the luxurious and ignorant do, the wise man also will do, but not in the same manner, and with the same purpose. Aristippus, the philosopher, defended his own immoralities by saying he committed them in a spirit differing from that of the really immoral. So the criticism of Cicero [1] was just; —that the disputations of the philosophers, though containing most abundant fountains of virtue and knowledge, when compared with their practice, seemed to be rather a pleasant occupation to pass the time,

[1] Lact. Div. Inst. iii. 16.

than advantage in the business of life. The verdict of Aristides[1] was fully borne out when he said:— "Their greediness is insatiable, their pillage of others' property they call community of goods; their envy is nicknamed philosophy, they call beggary, contempt of money. Haughty to all others, they creep before the rich, nay, before the very cooks and bakers of the rich. Their strength lies in impudence, and asking, in abuse, and in calumny." And again, Quintilian, " In our days most people hide their worst vices under the names of old philosophers."[2]

Besides all this the philosophers were not agreed amongst themselves. There was no necessity for the Christians to refute them, they refuted one another. Their teaching was nothing but a confused babble of conflicting voices. Lactantius[3] describes them as mad with the desire of contradiction. The disciples of one school condemned all others as false and vain, and they armed themselves for battle, neither knowing what they ought to defend or what to refute; and they made attacks everywhere, without distinction, upon all the views of their opponents.

Of course, the consequence was, their teaching had no power to influence the masses, who require a guide speaking with authority and clearness. And, indeed, philosophy did not address itself to the many, but to the rich who could afford a fee, or to the well-educated in science, or to those capable of abstract thought.[4] As for all the rest they were looked down upon in

---

[1] Quoted by Döllinger, ii. 157.   [2] Ib. ii. 157.
[3] Div. Inst. vii. 7.   [4] Just. Dial. c. 2.

contempt, and left to their irrational superstition. They were as the people who knew not the Law amongst the Jews. Even to its disciples philosophy was not a practical guide. The questions it discussed were words and names. It did not speak to the heart, or to the senses, but only to the intellect of a man. It enunciated certain laws, but they were based on no rewards or punishments. It was a school of opinions, not a discipline of life.[1]

And if to the Stoic philosophers many of these criticisms do not apply, if there were amongst them many who spoke to the conscience and heart, still remonstrances of vice were more common with them than exhortations to virtue. They uttered them, despairing of any good result. Their teaching, no less than that of the other philosophers, was utterly unfit for the many, and the basis of their morality was pride.[2]

Against these slight aims and slighter results of philosophy, its partial application and its unpractical nature, the Apologists contrasted the Christian revelation; of divine nature and origin; speaking with authority and consistency; appealing to all, learned and unlearned, rich and poor, young and old; in its very essence practical, for those ceased to be Christians in name who were not Christians in life. They have an Example of virtue, they have rewards of virtue. Their morality is based not on pride but on love. They have learned the truth, God has revealed it to them.

[1] See Merivale, 'Conversion of Roman Empire,' p. 94, &c.
[2] Döllinger, 'Jew and Gentile,' ii. 125.

The Apologists find some germs of truth in the writings of the philosophers, and they explain the fact in various ways. Sometimes they charge them with borrowing from the Hebrew prophets;[1] Plato especially is accused of borrowing from Moses.[2] Others say the demons inspired them with their knowledge. But the most beautiful account is given by Justin.[3] He had in turn tried all the principal systems of philosophy, and insufficient as they were to satisfy him, he still retained them in his affection. He loved to see in them the germs of Christianity, and to see in Christianity their full development. He was not satisfied with viewing Christianity alone; he viewed it in relation to all other systems. The Incarnation of Christ was to him the centre point of history, to which all the teaching of Prophets and philosophers converged, from which all truth radiated. God had never left Himself without a witness; He had been working in the minds of men who knew Him not by name. All this was done by His Word. The Incarnate Word brought to their full development those truths of which the Seminal Word had been depositing the germ. All men, he believed, had been partakers of the Word. The proof of this lay in the lives of men. Not all were partakers alike; the communication was according to capacity. The demons hate and persecute all who have in any manner been partakers of The Word.

Not all the Apologists can see so much to admire

---

[1] Tert. Apol. c. 47.
[2] Just. Hort. c. 26, 29, 31; Just. Apol. i. 59, 60.
[3] Apol. i. 46, ii. 7-10, 13.

in the philosophic system. Tertullian especially regards it as a thing utterly alien from Christ and Christians.[1] He never refers to it except to denounce it. Its wisdom can do nothing but corrupt. He asks, "Is there any likeness between the Christian and the philosopher? Between the disciple of Greece and the disciple of Heaven? Between the man whose object is fame and the man whose object is life? Between the talker and the doer? Between the man who builds up and the man who pulls down? Between the friend and the foe of error? Between one who corrupts the truth and one who restores and teaches it? Between its thief and its guardian?"

Tertullian looks at philosophy from its practical side and in his narrow spirit, and he can see nothing but its defects. To those who realize the truth of St. John's teaching, that The Word "was the true Light which lighteth every man that cometh into the world,"[2] Justin's theory will appear to be nearer the truth. Still we have seen enough to assure us also of the truth of St. Paul's words, "The world by wisdom knew not God."[3]

Lactantius[4] gives to us a very apt conclusion to this chapter. "The sum of the matter is this: the unlearned and the foolish esteem false religions as true, because they neither know the true nor understand the false. But the more sagacious, because they are ignorant of the true, either persist in those religions which they know to be false, that they may appear to possess something; or worship nothing at all, that they may not fall into error; whereas this very thing partakes largely of error, under the figure of a man to imitate the life of cattle. To understand that which is false, is truly the part of wisdom, but of human wisdom. Beyond this step the man cannot proceed, and thus many of the philosophers have taken away religious institutions, as I have pointed out; but to know the truth is the part of divine wisdom. But man of himself cannot attain to this knowledge unless he is taught by God."

CHAPTER VI.

CHRISTIANS AND CHRISTIANITY.

WE come now to the Apologists' description of Christians and Christianity. We must, now as before, bear in mind their object; namely, to defend themselves, not to convince the heathen. Their appeal is, Put a stop to the persecutions; not, Become Christians. So their account of themselves and their religion is mainly intended to answer accusations and misrepresentations. They could best show what they were not, by describing what they were.

We have already noticed the Apologetic account of the heathen deities; let us now contrast with it Tertullian's description[1] of the Christians' God. "The object of our worship is the One God; He who by His commanding word, His arranging wisdom, His mighty power, brought forth from nothing this entire mass of the world, with all its array of elements, bodies, and spirits, for the glory of His majesty; whence also the Greeks have bestowed on it the name of Cosmos (order). The eye cannot see Him, though He is visible. He is incomprehensible, though in grace He is manifested. He is beyond our utmost thought, though our human

[1] Apol. c. 17.

faculties conceive of Him. He is therefore equally real and great. That which, in an ordinary way, can be seen, and handled, and estimated, is inferior to the eyes by which it is taken in, and the hands by which it is touched, and the faculties by which it is discovered; but that which is infinite is known to itself. Hence we are enabled to make an estimate of God, while at the same time He does not admit of our estimation. Thus the force of His greatness presents Him to men, as at once known and unknown. And this is the crowning guilt of men, that they will not recognize one of whom they cannot possibly be ignorant."

The superiority of the Christian conception of God does not need pointing out; but it is worth while noticing that Tertullian is defining his position against both classes of his antagonists. As against votaries of the religion of the gods he says, God is incomprehensible, God is infinitely great. As against the philosophers he says, God *is*, and He is manifested. We know *something* concerning Him, though we cannot know all.

We notice next the Apologetic teaching concerning God's Providence. In no particular is the superiority of the Christian religion to the heathen more clearly to be seen, than in its conception of God's dealings with mankind.

The heathen deities did, indeed, concern themselves with the affairs of earth, being in fact men on a larger and more powerful scale; they came and meddled and tyrannized amongst men in much the same way as a few big boys might in a school of little ones;

like them, taking opposite sides in any dispute, utterly unreasonable in their likes and dislikes, and thwarting each other to the best of their power. But they were confessedly not all-powerful beings. There was a power above them of which they were conscious, but whose dealings were so little understood that they gave it no form.[1] Against this abstract power, which they called Fate, it was useless to struggle,—gods and men were alike powerless in its hands. Christianity came in with its flood of light and transformed the abstract Fate into a personal God,[2] who watched over His creatures with all the tenderness of a Father, and all the power of an Almighty Being. The heathen never imagined that close personal attention extending to thoughts and words, that ever-watchful, ever-present care which the Christian represented his God as exercising over the affairs of men. Such ideas appeared to him absurd.[3] In the language of the heathen in the Octavius of Minucius Felix,[4] "What strange and portentous imaginations do the Christians form to themselves concerning their Deity! that this God of theirs, whom they cannot show to others, nor themselves see, carefully examines into the dispositions of all men, and into the behaviour of all men, and even into their words and most secret thoughts. They describe Him as continually running hither and thither, and as present everywhere; as a Being, troublesome, restless, and immoderately inquisitive; who at all actions is a bystander, and who strays

---

[1] Tat. Orat. c. 8, 9; Arn. adv. Gentes, i. 34, vii. 10.
[2] Octavius, c. 36.   [3] Origen c. Celsum, iv. 99.
[4] Octavius, c. 10.

into every place; although it is impossible that He should regard particulars while attentive to the whole, or be sufficient for the whole while He is occupied about particulars."

The Christian replies,[1] "All things celestial and earthly are known to Him, and full of Him." "He is in all places most near to us; nay, He is infused into us all. Consider again the sun, fixed in heaven, and yet spread over the whole earth; he is equally present in all places, and blended with the whole creation, and everywhere his brightness remains inviolate. How much more is God, who made and who surveys all things,—how much more is He present in darkness, and present even in that profound darkness—our thoughts! We not only act under His inspection, but, I had almost said, we live with Him." "Neither let us men amuse ourselves with the fond hope of impunity because of our numbers. In our own sight we are many, but to God we appear very few. We make distinctions of peoples and countries, but to Him the whole world is as one house. Kings are not otherwise acquainted with the details of their dominions than by the ministration of nferi or officers; but God needs not to be informed of anything, for we live not only under His eyes, but in His bosom."

The heathen had, as we have seen, many gods; they gave to each god his own little work to do;[2] and yet they did not imagine that their gods, in their limited spheres, exercised that providential care, which

---

[1] Octavius, c. 32, 33.   [2] Orig. c. Celsum, vii. 70, viii. 58.

the Christian believed His one God exercised, in every single part of the whole universe.

"The Immortality of the Soul" and "the Resurrection of the Body" were doctrines put prominently forward by the Apologists. The former of these had been taught by some poets and philosophers, but it was not generally received or practically applied. The heathen, in the Octavius of Minucius Felix,[1] speaks of it as a fiction of a crazed fancy, and a foolish topic of consolation on which the poets have sported in melodious and deceitful verse. He argues that the God who will not or cannot aid his own in this life, cannot be able to restore men to life when dead. "It is madness," he says, "to promise immortality after death and extinction to us men, who, as we came into being, must also cease to be."

On the other hand, the Christians accepted these doctrines as the practical basis of their life, and as a sure ground of confidence in the hour of death. "We," says Tertullian,[2] "who receive our awards under the judgment of an all-seeing God, and who look forward to eternal punishment from Him for sin; we alone make real effort to attain a blameless life." "If we believed," says Athenagoras,[3] "that we should live only the present life, then we might be suspected of sinning; but since we are persuaded that, when we are removed from the present life, we shall live another life, better than the present one, and in heaven, or, perishing with the rest, a worse one, and in fire, it is not likely that we should wish to do evil, or deliver ourselves over to

---

[1] Octavius, c. 10, 11, 12.   [2] Apol. c. 45.   [3] Legat. c. 31.

the Great Judge to be punished." "After death I shall exist again," says Tatian.[1] "Even though you destroy all traces of my flesh, the world receives the vaporized matter; and though dispersed through rivers and seas, and torn in pieces by wild beasts, I am laid up in the storehouses of a wealthy Lord."

The Apologists use the argument from analogy to recommend the doctrine of the Resurrection of the Body to the heathen. The world bears in itself a witness, nay, the exact image of the resurrection. Light, every day extinguished, shines out again; and with like alternation, darkness comes and goes. The defunct stars re-live; the seasons, as soon as they are finished, renew their course; the fruits are brought to maturity, and are then reproduced. The seeds do not spring up with abundant produce, save as they rot and dissolve away; all things are preserved by perishing, all things are refashioned out of death. Thou, man, of nature so exalted, ... lord of all these things that die and rise, shalt thou die to perish evermore? Thus Tertullian,[2] and even still more beautifully, Minucius Felix:[3] "See, therefore, how for our consolation all nature suggests a future resurrection. The sun sinks in the ocean and emerges. The planets glide on in their course and come back; the flowers fall and live anew; after a temporary old age, the shrubs reassume their foliage; and seeds must be corrupted before they can put forth shoots. So is the body in the grave: it resembles trees, which in winter conceal their vegetation under a feigned appearance of withering. Why should you be impatient

[1] Orat. c. 6. [2] Apol. c. 48. [3] Octavius, c. 34.

for its revival and restoration while winter is yet intense? We must await the spring-time of the body."

Passing on to the doctrines exclusively Christian, we find the Apologists clearly stating who the founder of their religion is. "Our teacher of these things," says Justin,[1] "is Jesus Christ, who also was born for this purpose, and was crucified under Pontius Pilate, procurator of Judæa, in the times of Tiberius Cæsar; and we reasonably worship Him, having learned He is the Son of the true God Himself." "We Christians," says Arnobius, "are nothing else than worshippers of the Supreme King and Head, under our Master, Christ. If you examine carefully, you will find that nothing else is implied in our religion. This is the sum of all that we do; this is the proposed end and limit of our sacred duties. Before Him we all prostrate ourselves, according to our custom; Him we adore in united prayers; from Him we beg things just and honourable, and worthy of His ear."[2]

Amongst the various titles of our Lord perhaps "The Word" is the one most commonly used by the Apologists. They describe His work as the revelation of God to man, and the restitution of truth to men.[3] The deeper mysteries concerning sin and atonement were kept hidden from the profane gaze. Naturally, also, they touch but seldom on the doctrines of His Person and Nature. Such discussions would have been out of place in Apologies addressed

[1] Apol. i. c. 13.   [2] Adv. Gentes, i. 27.
[3] Tert. Apol. c. 21; Just. Apol. ii. 6, 10, 13; Lact. Div. Inst. iv. 8.

to unbelievers. As vindication for their own conduct in taking Him as their Master and Teacher, they give three reasons,—the wisdom and morality of His words and deeds, ancient prophecies concerning Him, and miracles wrought by Him.

The first of these was easily stated, and could be easily grasped, and, without doubt, came home to many thoughtful heathen hearts. Many who did not acknowledge Christ as their Lord, did homage to the beauty of His character, the purity of His teaching, and the beneficence of His life. Tiberius is said to have wished to enrol Christ amongst the gods.[1] On one occasion the oracles were consulted by Pagans whether Christ might be worshipped along with the other gods.[2] They answered, "He who is wise knows that the soul rises immortal from the body; but the soul of that man is pre-eminent in piety." When they were asked why Christ suffered death, the answer was, "To be subject to light sufferings is always the lot of the body, but the soul of the pious rises to the fields of heaven." Porphyry takes occasion to say that Christ must not be calumniated, though he condemns those who worship Him.[3] The Emperor Alexander Severus[4] had a bust of Christ in his Lararium. He intended to have caused Christ to be enrolled amongst the Roman deities; and he constantly repeated the words of Christ: "As ye would that men should do to you, do ye also to them likewise." The purity of Christ's teaching and life was then a fact acknow-

---
[1] Tert. Apol. c. 5.
[2] Cf. Neander, 'History of Church,' i. 239.
[3] Neander, ib.   [4] Ib. i. 173.

ledged by many heathen. The Apologists make use of this.[1] They often point out that so pure a teacher is hardly likely to have as his followers those practising the worst of crimes. They show how His teaching extended more deeply than that of any other to the words and thoughts of men. "We alone," says Tertullian,[2] "are without crime. Is there anything wonderful in that, if it be a very necessity with us? For a necessity it is. Taught of God Himself what goodness is, we have a perfect knowledge of it as revealed to us by a perfect Master." The Christian idea of virtue, he remarks, did not rest on human opinion, nor was it a matter of human obligation. And which, he asks, was the ampler rule, "To say, 'Thou shalt not kill,' or to teach, 'Be not even angry'?" Which is more perfect, to forbid adultery, or to restrain from even a single lustful look? Which indicates the higher intelligence, interdicting evil-doing or evil-speaking? Which is more thorough, not allowing an injury, or not even suffering an injury done to you to be repaid?"

Very commonly the Apologists appeal to the evidence of Prophecy in their vindication of the claims of Christ to be a teacher sent from God. They allege predictions of undoubted antiquity spread over hundreds of years, and show their fulfilment in the life, and death, and work of Jesus Christ. This argument was far more subtle than the former one, and required great discrimination in its use. The Apologists cannot be said to have had the discrimination necessary.

[1] Just. Apol. i. c. 15-17; Athenagoras, c. 32-35.
[2] Tert. Apol. c. 45.

They always seem to approach the subject from their stand-point of believers. They do not seem at all able to distinguish between those prophecies which could serve only to comfort and instruct a man who has already accepted the truth, and those which might convince an unbeliever of the truth. Justin Martyr is a great offender in this respect. In his Dialogue[1] with the Jew Trypho he proves that the twelve bells attached to the robes of the high-priest were types of the twelve Apostles, and then goes on to remark, " In short, by enumerating the other appointments of Moses, I can demonstrate that they were types, and symbols, and declarations of those things which would happen to Christ, of those who, it was foreknown, were to believe in Him, and of those things which would also be done by Christ Himself."

Origen is perhaps the most cautious in selecting his proofs from prophecy; but no Apologist is very happy in the statement of this part of his case. It may indeed be doubted whether it was wise in them to enter into any prophetical details. For the due appreciation of the evidence, research, conscientious beyond all expectation, on the part of those whom they addressed, was required, and an examination of books accessible only to Jews. It was quite competent for them to appeal generally to the evidence of the ancient books of the Old Testament.[2] The Septuagint translation had made them comparatively widely known, and the Jews were the guardians of their integrity. It was

[1] Dialogue, c. 42.
[2] So Tertullian, Apol. c. 19; Justin, Apol. i. c. 31; Theophilus, Letters ii. and iii.; Tatian, c. 29.

quite competent for them to point out the consistency and harmony, the accuracy and extent of the revelation therein contained. They could, if they pleased, claim, in general terms, that Jesus of Nazareth was He whom the prophets said would come, and rule, and save. Thus doing, they would have given their religion that antiquity which it wanted in the popular idea.[1] But it is probable that, in going further, they wasted their time and energy, and defeated their purpose, by giving arguments beyond ordinary grasp. It was quite understood, and practically carried out by many of the Apologists, that in their works testimonies from Scripture were out of place.[2] The words of Lactantius[3] are well worth recording. "Cyprian," he says, "when endeavouring to refute Demetrian, did not handle his subject as he ought to have done; for he (Demetrian) ought to have been refuted, not by the testimonies of Scripture, which he plainly considered vain, fictitious, and false, but by arguments and reason. For, since he (Cyprian) was contending against a man who was ignorant of the truth, he ought for a while to have laid aside divine readings, and to have built up from the beginning this man as one who was altogether ignorant, and to have shown to him by degrees the beginnings of light, that he might not be dazzled by the whole of its brightness being presented to him."

The argument from the miracles of Christ was not

---

[1] Ep. to Diognetus, c. i.; Theophilus, Letter iii. 4; Arnobius, i. 24: cf. also a decree of Diocletian.

[2] Cf. Tertullian's Apology, but not Justin's.

[3] Div. Inst. v. 4.

at first so commonly used as we might have expected. Miracles were commonly ascribed to magic, and magicians were not men likely to obtain the respect of any. To appeal to Christ's miracles was to be met by the retort that He was a magician and imposter.[1] The later Apologists deal with the question. Lactantius[2] says that magic has no power except to deceive the eyes. Origen, in answer to Celsus,[3] who had compared Christ's miracles to the tricks of jugglers, compares the objects and the agents in the two cases. The dealers in magical arts performed their works only for show, and in return for a few oboli. They never invited the spectators to reform their manners, and indeed their own lives were full of the grossest and most notorious sins. Christ, by His miracles, induced those who beheld them to change their lives, and He Himself was the pattern of a most virtuous life. Arnobius draws clearly and thoroughly the distinction between Christ's miracles and those of all others.[4] He is answering the charge that Jesus was a magician, and an adept at secret arts stolen from Egypt. He asks what magician has ever, even in the thousandth degree, worked miracles like Him? The magicians work by the power of incantations, the juice of herbs and grasses, the anxious watching of sacrifices and seasons, and by the invocation of deities. Christ

---

[1] The fragment extant of the Apology of Quadratus, the first Apologist, shows that he distinguished between Christ's miracles and those of others. Cf. Eus. H. E. iv. 3.
[2] Div. Inst. iv. 15. [3] C. Celsum, i. 68.
[4] Adv. Gentes, i. 43-55. (This, as in other places, is Arnobius's language compressed.)

worked without any aid from external things, without the observance of any ceremonial, without any fixed mode of procedure, and by the might of His inherent power. The deeds of the magicians were useless and harmful. They consisted in the infliction of diseases, the stirring of discord, the revealing of secrets, the "getting at" (to use a modern phrase) horses, the exciting unlawful love by philtres. Christ did nothing hurtful or injurious, but only that which was helpful and full of blessings to men. Was He one of us, he asks, at whose voice infirmities and diseases of the body fled away? Was He one of us, whose very sight the race of demons was unable to bear? Was He one of us, at whose word the raging and maddened seas were still, who walked over the deepest pools with unwet foot, who with five loaves satisfied five thousand of His followers? Was He one of us, who ordered the breath that had departed to return to the body? Was He one of us, who saw clearly in the hearts of the silent what each was pondering? Was He one of us, who, after His body had been laid in the tomb, manifested Himself in open day to countless numbers of men? Was He one of us, who appears even now to righteous men of pure mind who love Him, whose name when heard puts to flight evil spirits, silences the soothsayers, and frustrates the magicians? Was He one of us, who conquered those decrees of fate to which even the gods are subject? Compare Him not with your deities. The comparison will not hold. They have at times relieved disease by medicine; the credit is due to the drug, not to the giver. They have, it is said, healed a few; but how many thousands, life-long suppliants, have been sent empty away! Christ ordered diseases to fly from men at a touch and a word. Christ healed all who came to Him, good and bad alike. And more wonderful still, He communicated His powers to others, and to whom? fishermen, artisans, rustics, and unskilled persons of a similar kind. He gave them the power to do all things which He had done.

What say ye? O minds incredulous, stubborn, hardened! Did that great Jupiter Capitolinus of yours give to any human being power of this kind? Did he endow with this right any Pontifex Maximus? To be able to transfer to a man your own power, to share with the frailest being the ability to perform that which you alone are able to do, is a proof of power, supreme over all, and holding in subjection the causes of all things, and the natural laws of methods and of means. Cease in your ignorance to receive such great deeds with abusive language. There was nothing magical in Christ. He was God on high, sent by the Ruler of all things as the Saviour God. But you do not believe these things. Yet eye-witnesses believed them, and transmitted their belief. If the record is false, how is it the belief has spread? How is it that nations dwelling widely apart unite in one conclusion? They have been prevailed upon (you say) by vain hopes and mere assertions to run voluntarily the risks of death. Nay, was it not because they had seen these things? Was it not because the force of truth had overcome them, that they devoted themselves to God, and reckoned it but a small sacrifice to surrender their bodies to you?

Thus conclusively, by a comparison of the means used, results achieved, universality of success, transmission of the power, and the enthusiastic and practical belief which they inspired, does Arnobius prove the superiority of the miracles of Christ.

When the Apologists are comparing the religion of Christ with the religion of the gods, they have no more legitimate ground for boasting than the moral results the profession of Christianity produced. Over and over again they appeal to the purity of Christian lives as a proof of the truth of the Christian faith. The close connection, it must be remembered, between morality and religion, which seems to us so obvious, was not obvious to the heathen mind. On the contrary, gross immoralities were connected with the worship of the gods; and the rule of faith was quite dissevered from the rule of life. Lactantius, the latest Apologist, brings home most clearly this fact. "The worship of God," he says, "of all things requires the greatest devotedness and fidelity. How can God love the worshipper, if He Himself is not loved by him? How can He grant the petitioner his request if he draw nigh without sincerity or reverence? You heathen," he says, "present your gods with nothing from within, no uprightness of mind, no reverence or fear. When your worthless sacrifices are completed, you leave your religion altogether in the temple where you found it. You took no religion there, and you take none away. So your religious observances are not able to make men good, or to be permanent in themselves. Men are easily led away from them, because they teach nothing as to conduct, or as to wisdom, or as to faith. For what is the religion of the gods? What is its power? What is its discipline? What its origin? What its principles? What its foundation? What its substance? What its tendency? What its hope? There is nothing in it that cannot be learned by rule of thumb. On the other hand, our religion is firm, and solid, and unchangeable, because it has its existence in the soul of the worshipper, because it has the mind of man itself for a sacrifice. In the heathen religion nothing is required but the blood of animals, and the smoke of incense, and the senseless pouring out of libations. In ours is required a good mind, a pure breast, an innocent life. The heathen rites are frequented by harlots, gladiators, robbers, thieves, and sorcerers, who pray for nothing else but that they may commit crimes with impunity. But in our religion there is no place even for a slight and ordinary offence; and if any one shall come to a sacrifice without a sound conscience, he hears what threats God denounces against him; that God, I say, who sees the secret places of the heart, who is always hostile to sin, who requires justice, who demands fidelity. What place is there here for an evil mind or for an evil prayer? The unhappy heathen do not understand how evil it is to worship when stained by sin. They imagine that they offer a pious sacrifice if they wash their skin, as though any stream could wash away, or any seas purify, the lusts shut up within the breast. How much better it would be to cleanse the mind defiled by evil desires, and to drive away all vices by the one laver of virtue and faith. He who shall do this, although he have a body defiled with sin, is sufficiently pure."

It was of course the fact that worship was not a mere ritual observance, but the offering up of the whole man, body, soul, and spirit, to his God, that made Christians so determined in their refusal to join in any of the idolatrous ceremonies. The heathen were utterly unable to understand their obstinacy, as the records of all the persecutions show. It seemed to them utter folly to choose "to be tortured and slain rather than to take incense in three fingers and throw it upon the hearth"[1] "They do not know," says Lactantius, "how great an act of impiety it is to adore any other object than God, who made heaven and earth, who fashioned the human race, who breathed into them the breath of life, and gave them light. If he is accounted the most worthless of slaves who runs away and deserts his master, and if he is judged most deserving of stripes, and chains, and a prison, and the cross, and all evil; if a son likewise is thought abandoned, and impious, and worthy of being disinherited, who deserts his father, how much more does he who forsakes God, in whom the two names entitled to equal reverence of Lord and Father alike meet!"

Animated with this intense devotion to their God, the Christians did not fear what man could do unto them. "With a fury more insatiable than that of wild beasts," says Lactantius,[2] "you rage against us. When

[1] Lact. Div. Inst. v. 19.   [2] Ib. v. 11.

their appetite is satisfied they rest in peace. You, with iron teeth, ever rage throughout the world. You are not content with tearing in pieces the limbs of men, you break their bones, and rage over their ashes, so that there may be no place for their burial. You deny light to the living, earth to the dead. Death is too merciful a thing for you. Some of you contend how you may conquer by inflicting exquisite pain, and you avoid nothing else, except only that the victims may not die under the torture. You carefully tend the tortured in order that they may be capable of enduring fresh tortures. One of you was elated with joy because a victim who had resisted for two years with great spirit appeared at length to yield. Can you not see that it is not foolishness, but wisdom, which causes us to be thus steadfast in suffering? It is not one place, or one sex, or one age, which furnishes examples of endurance. Everywhere there is the same patient endurance, the same contempt of death. There must be some foundation for that religion which thus thrives under persecution. Robbers and strong men with you cannot bear similar torture, but amongst us not even boys and delicate women are overcome. You may boast in your Mucius, who laid his hand upon the burning hearth as an atonement for his crime. You may boast of your Regulus, who gave himself up to death rather than live a life of shame. But our weak women and our slender boys endure laceration in the whole body, and not even the fire can extort from them a groan. They could escape if they so wished; they voluntarily endure all because they put their trust in

God. And what is the result of all these persecutions? Our numbers are increased.[1] Some hate cruelty and are drawn to us. Some are pleased with virtue and faith. Some suspect that there must be evil in that worship which we abjure at the cost of life. Some desire to know what that good is which we prefer to all the joys of life, and from which no loss of goods, no bodily pain, deters us. In the midst of your torments we tell the bystanders that sacrifices are not due to stocks and stones, graven by art or man's device, but to the living God who is in heaven. Many, when they hear, believe it to be true. A fresh crowd is added to us, because of the wonderful nature of the virtue displayed."[2]

The same religion which made Christians thus faithful to their God, and thus patient in enduring persecution, also made them just and kind to their fellow-men. They reckoned themselves, as children of one Father, to be all equal in the sight of God. None was poor but he that was without justice; none rich but he who was full of virtues. The excellent were the good and innocent; the renowned, those who were most merciful. To the question, "Are there not among you Christians some poor, and others rich, some servants, and others masters?" the answer was, "There is no difference between one man and another. Why should we call one another brethren, except we reckoned ourselves to be equal? In lowliness of mind we are all on an equality, the free with slaves, and the rich with the poor, nevertheless in the sight of

---

[1] Lact. Div. Inst. v. 23.   [2] Ib. v. 13.

God we are distinguished in respect of virtue. Every one is more exalted according to his greater justice."

It is the life of holiness towards God, love towards their fellow-men, and patience under injury, to which Lactantius points as the sacrifice which God desires. "God does not desire," he says, "the sacrifice of a dumb animal, nor of death and blood, but of man and life.[1] In this sacrifice there is neither need of sacred boughs, nor of purifications, nor of sods of turf, which things are plainly most vain, but of those things which are put forth from the innermost breast. Therefore on the altar of God, which is truly great, and which is placed in the heart of man, and cannot be defiled with blood, there are placed righteousness, patience, faith, innocence, chastity, and abstinence. Spiritual gifts must be offered to God, who is a Spirit. His offering is innocency of soul, His sacrifice praise and a hymn. The worship of God consists of one thing,— not to be wicked."

But perhaps it will be said, that it is impossible, if the Christians had been so pure and lovely in character, they would have been so intensely hated. And yet our Lord is a convincing proof to the contrary. We know also that "he that doeth evil hateth the light, neither cometh to the light, lest his deeds should be reproved." Wicked men search diligently for bad motives to good actions. That was the case with many heathen in the first three centuries. They tried to account for the Christians' lives and deaths, and they came to the conclusion that a senseless

---

[1] Ib. vi. 24.

enthusiasm and wicked superstition animated them.[1] When they had settled this to their own satisfaction, they gave them no reverence for their virtues, and despised them for their fanaticism. The objection may also be raised that this description of Christian lives and deaths comes from those who were Christian themselves, and that more impartial witnesses are needed. It is certainly important for us to know what the heathen of the first three centuries thought of the Christians, and so we shall give two descriptions of them from heathen sources. They are both made by philosophers, and neither of them appears to have been a man of moral worth.

The first description is that given by Lucian. It is contained in his account of the death of a certain Peregrinus, who was perhaps a real, perhaps only a fictitious, character. This Peregrinus was a traveller from place to place, and a wanderer from one sect of philosophy to another. He was obliged to leave his native country because of his crimes; and in the course of his travels he learned in Palestine the wonderful doctrine of the Christians. In a short time they were but children to him; he held all their offices —prophet, high priest, and ruler of a synagogue. He wrote some books for them and interpreted others. They called him a god, and took him for a lawgiver, and gave him the title of master. They were still worshippers of the great man who was crucified in Palestine—the founder of their religion; and for this reason Peregrinus was put in prison. He turned his

[1] Pliny; Lucian, de Morte Peregrini; Octavius, c. 11.

imprisonment to good account; the Christians were much grieved at it, and tried to procure his liberty in all ways. Not being able to effect that, they did him all sorts of kindnesses; and these, not casually, but with the greatest care. Early in the morning old women and little children would be at the prison gates. The chief men would spend the night with him; they had a supper together, and the sacred books were read. Even from Asia some Christians came commissioned to relieve, encourage, and comfort him. It is incredible what expedients they use when any of their friends are known to be in trouble. They spare nothing on such occasions; and so Peregrinus's chain brought him in a good sum of money. These miserable men have no doubt they are immortal; and they despise death, and surrender themselves to suffering. Their first lawgiver has taught them that, when they have forsaken the gods of the Greeks, and worship Him, and engage to live according to His law, they are all brethren. They despise the things of the world, and regard them as common, and trust one another without security. Any subtle fellow can impose upon them,—so simple are they. Peregrinus was ultimately liberated from prison; he was provided with money for his travelling expenses, and he lived in great plenty. So it went on for some time. At last he separated from them; he had given them offence, as Lucian supposes, by eating some forbidden food. Remembering what Lucian was,—a scoffer at all religions and a licentious wit,—is it not matter of pride that he has nothing worse to say of us than this? Have we not a most beautiful picture of faith, hope, and love shining forth in Christian life? And may we not triumph in the thought that the subtle, worthless philosopher, reverenced as a god forsooth, and ministered to with such undeserved kindness, was found out in the end by the simple people whom he had deceived?

And now for another picture of Christians painted by a heathen: this we shall find to be of quite a different character. It is painted by the philosopher Celsus, and it is to be found in his own words in Origen's answer to him.[1]

He compares Jews and Christians together "to a flight of bats, or a swarm of ants issuing out of their nest, or to frogs holding council in a marsh, or to worms crawling together in the corner of a dunghill, and quarrelling with one another as to which of them are the greater sinners, and asserting that God shows and announces to us all things beforehand; and that, abandoning the whole world, and the regions of heaven, and this great earth, He becomes a citizen among us alone; and to us alone makes His intimations, and does not cease sending and inquiring in what way we may be associated with Him for ever."[2] "It is only foolish and low individuals, and persons devoid of perception, and slaves, and women, and children, of whom the teachers of the Divine Word wish to make converts."[3] They have laid down as a rule, "Let no one come to us who has been instructed, or who is wise or prudent (for such qualifications are deemed evil by us); but if there be any ignorant, or

---

[1] Origen c. Celsum, iv. 23. [2] Ib. iii. 49. [3] Ib. iii. 44.

unintelligent, or uninstructed, or foolish persons, let them come with confidence." Thus "they manifestly show that they desire and are able to gain over only the silly, and the mean, and the stupid, with women and children." Others invite to participation in their mysteries those of clean hands and a pure tongue; but the Christians say, "Every one who is a sinner, who is devoid of understanding, who is a child, and, to speak generally, whoever is unfortunate, him will the kingdom of God receive." "What others would a man invite if he were issuing a proclamation for an assembly of robbers?"[1] They are like "the jugglers who gather crowds around them in the market-places, but who never dare to approach an assembly of wise men, or dare to exhibit their arts among them."[2] "They act insolently towards God, in order to lead on wicked men by empty hopes, and to persuade them to despise better things.[3] They are a set of people associated together contrary to law.[4] Their religion is barbarous in origin and secret in practice.[5] Their system of morals is not new, and their miracles are worked in the names of certain demons, and by the use of incantations.[6] Like the devil-worshippers, they take advantage of the ignorance of those who are easily deceived. They do not wish either to give or receive a reason for their belief, but keep repeating, 'Do not examine, but believe.' 'Your faith will save you.' 'The wisdom of this life is bad, and foolishness is a good thing.'[7] At first, being few in number, they held the same opinions, but when

[1] Origen c. Celsum, iii. 59.　[2] Ib. iii. 50.　[3] Ib. iii. 78.
[4] Ib. i. 1.　[5] Ib. i. 2.　[6] Ib. i. 4.　[7] Ib. i. 9.

they grew to be a great multitude, they were divided and separated, each wishing to have his own party.[1] They differ from one another widely, and assail one another in their disputes with the most shameful language, and yet they say, 'The world is crucified unto me and I unto the world.'[2] If all were like them, kings would be left in utter solitude and desertion, and the affairs of the earth would fall into the hands of the wildest and most lawless barbarians; and then there would no longer remain among men any of the glory of their religion, or of the true wisdom.[3] If they refuse to render due service to the gods, and to respect those who are set over this service, let them not come to manhood, or marry wives, or have children, or, indeed, take any share in the affairs of life; but let them depart hence with all speed and leave no posterity behind them, that such a race may become extinct from the face of the earth."[4]

Such is Celsus's description, or rather caricature of Christians and Christianity. There is very little in it to trouble us. It is sad, indeed, to see the divisions of Christians already attracting the attention of heathen. Perhaps, too, there are indications that the teachers of the gospel were not always careful enough to show the reasonableness of their faith; and that the believers of the gospel sometimes neglected their duties as citizens in the State. But most of the reproaches cast by Celsus are our glory. We rejoice to hear that the spiritually sick came to Christ, for in their healing His power was magnified. We rejoice to

[1] Origen c. Celsum, iii. 10.   [2] Ib. v. 64.
[3] Ib. viii. 68.   [4] Ib. viii. 55.

hear that the Christian religion attracted all kinds of men. We rejoice to see that the Christians reckoned all else as dross for the excellency of the knowledge of Christ Jesus their Lord. Celsus, it is plain, saw no beauty in the Christian character or in the Christian religion. That need not trouble us, for he saw no beauty in Christ our Lord. "If they have called the Master of the house Beelzebub, how much more shall they call them of His household."[1] Celsus can see no beauty or dignity in the Incarnation.[2] In Christ's deeds there was nothing truly great or worthy of a God.[3] His sufferings were only a proof of His weakness. His denial and betrayal by His own followers, and His punishment as a malefactor, were an utter refutation of His claims.[4] He does not even allow that Christ was a virtuous man.[5] He describes Him as "gathering round Himself ten or eleven persons of notorious character, the very wickedest of tax-gatherers and sailors, fleeing in company with them from place to place, and obtaining His living in a shameful and importunate manner." He says that the Christians set up "as a God one who ended a most infamous life by a most miserable death."[6] If he could thus misrepresent and misconceive Christ, what wonder is it if he slanders the Christian faith and Christian men. Still his misrepresentations have a value for us, for they show us how Christianity and Christians were regarded by some at least of their

---

[1] Matt. x. 25. [2] Origen c. Celsum, i. 28, iv. 23.
[3] Ib. ii. 30, 31, 33. [4] Ib. ii. 9, 12, 20.
[5] Ib. i. 62. [6] Ib. vii. 53.

heathen contemporaries; and we are better able to realize the nature of the opposition against which the Apologists had to contend.

We now proceed to the last point in the Apologetic description of Christianity on which we shall touch; viz. the Christian Worship. It will be remembered that the heathen viewed with the greatest suspicion the nocturnal assemblies of the Christians. They were thought to be scenes of gross immorality, and the meeting-places of conspirators against the rulers in the State. Two of the Apologists, Justin and Tertullian, endeavour to remove these suspicions by describing them as they really were. Justin's account is as follows.[1] Those who are persuaded and believe that what we teach and say is true, and undertake to live accordingly, are taught to beseech God with fasting and prayer; and we pray and fast along with them. Then they are brought by us where there is water, and are regenerated by the washing of water, in the name of God the Father and Lord of the Universe, and of our Saviour Jesus Christ, and of the Holy Spirit. For Christ also said, 'Except ye be born again, ye shall not enter into the kingdom of heaven.' This washing is called illumination, because they who learn these things are illuminated in their understandings. The baptized person is then brought into the assembly of our brethren,[2] in order that we may offer hearty prayers in common for ourselves and the newly baptized, and all others in every place, that we may be counted worthy, now that we have learned

---

[1] Just. Apol. i. 61. [2] Ib. i. 65.

the truth, to be found by our works also good citizens and keepers of the commandments, so that we may be saved with an everlasting salvation. Having ended the prayers, we salute one another with a kiss. Then to the President bread and a cup of wine mixed with water are brought. He takes them, and gives praise and glory to the Father through the name of the Son and the Holy Ghost, and offers thanks for our being counted worthy to receive these things at his hands. When he has concluded, all present say, Amen. Then the deacons distribute the consecrated bread and wine mixed with water, and carry away portions to the absent.[1] This food is called Eucharist, and is only for those who believe and are baptized, and are living a Christian life. Not as common bread and wine do we receive it, but as the flesh and blood of the Incarnate Jesus, and in accordance with His command.[2] We continually remind one another of these things. And on Sunday we gather together, and the memoirs of the Apostles and the writings of the prophets are read, and afterwards the President instructs and exhorts. Prayers, thanksgivings, and the Communion follow. Every one gives alms according to his own will. The President distributes the money collected amongst the orphans and widows, the sick and the needy, the prisoners and the strangers.

Tertullian does not add much to this account.[3] He is endeavouring to show that the assemblies of the Christians are in no sense factious or treasonable. So he tells the heathen the prayers were made with

---

[1] Just. Apol. i. 66. [2] Ib. i. 67. [3] Apol. c. 39.

united force for the Emperor and all in authority. Besides this, he tells us the Sacred Scriptures were read, exhortations made, rebukes and sacred censures administered. The offertory in his time was monthly. It was quite voluntary. There was no compulsion whatsoever. There was no buying or selling of any sort in the things of God. The money was used, not for feasting, but for the burial of the poor, the education of orphan children, the support of the old, and the assistance of those suffering for the truth's sake. The Christian feast (the Agape) permitted no vileness or immodesty. It began and ended with prayer. There was no such thing as immoderate eating and drinking. When the cravings of hunger were satisfied, hymns were sung by each in turn to God. Such a meeting, Tertullian thinks, ought not to be called a faction, but a Curia, a sacred meeting.

CHAPTER VII.

THE GREEK APOLOGISTS.

As we have already observed, the Christian Apologists of the second century wrote in Greek, those of the third century in Latin.[1] This difference of language and of time implies, of course, other differences also. The Greek Apologists spoke as Greeks; the Latin Apologists, though not Italians but Africans, spoke as citizens of the Roman empire. By the Greek Apologist the world is divided into two classes, Greeks and Barbarians. It is the Greek mythology which is exposed, the Greek philosophy which is refuted, the Greek writings which are compared with the Hebrew and Christian. But when we get to the Latin Apologists, the Romans everywhere appear as masters of the world. Roman history is appealed to, and Roman authors quoted. Moreover, Christianity was scarcely known to the authorities of the Empire when the *first* Apologists wrote. The Emperor was a Christian (so to speak) by conviction, though not by baptism, before the *last*. Many mistakes had been rectified in the mean time. No one thought at the beginning of the fourth century that the Christians were monsters of immorality. In the second century

---

[1] There is only one exception—Origen—to this rule.

this was the popular belief. On the other hand, no one imagined at first that the Christians would ever be able to accomplish their purpose of supplanting all the religions of the gods. They were considered by the authorities at that time to be a troublesome but not a dangerous people. In the third century the State found out they were far too powerful to be despised and ignored, and that there really was a probability that they might succeed in their efforts to subvert the State religion. The general feeling was, that, when the State religion fell, the State would fall too, so closely were the two things connected together. So the political charge took a prominent place. Of course the Apologists recognized this altered condition of things, and suited their defence to the attack. The charge of immorality appears in all the Greek Apologists except Clement of Alexandria, but only in two of the Latin, and those the earliest in date.[1] In the Greek Apologists, the political charges are very little touched upon; in the Latin, they are reckoned to be worthy of the chief attention. In the Greek Apologists, the charge of atheism is refuted; in the Latin, the charge of forsaking the worship of the gods.

And, besides this, the characteristics of the literature of Greece and Rome are to be discerned in either class. "On the one side there is universality, freedom, large sympathy, deep feeling; on the other, there is individuality, system, order, logic. The tendency of one mind is towards truth; of the other, towards law."[2]

[1] Tertullian, Minucius Felix.
[2] Quoted from Westcott's 'Canon,' c. ii. p. 59.

Or, quoting the same author, "The Greek Apologists show in what way Christianity was the satisfaction of all the deepest wants of humanity, the sum of all knowledge; it was reserved for the Latin Apologists to apprehend its independent claims, and establish its right to supplant, as well as to fulfil, what was partial and vague in earlier systems."[1] This last remark cannot be better illustrated than by comparing the relations of Justin and Tertullian with the heathen philosophy. Attention has been already drawn to this point in Chapter V. Justin reckons the philosophers, or at least some of them, to be Christians before Christ. Tertullian will have nothing to do with the teaching of the poets and philosophers.[2] He is willing to let it be granted that there is nothing in heathen writers which a Christian approves.

We proceed now to consider the separate "Apologies," and their writers. Sometimes we shall give abstracts of, or striking passages in, the writings, sometimes incidents in the lives and deaths of the writers.

JUSTIN MARTYR. 110–165 A.D. CIRCA.

The earliest extant "Apologies" are those of Justin. He was born early in the 2nd century, and suffered martyrdom during the reign of Marcus Aurelius, A.D. 165. His life gives us valuable information on the relations of Christianity with

---

[1] Westcott's 'Canon,' c. ii. p. 56.
[2] De Testim. Animæ,' c. i.

the philosophers and the Roman State. He himself studied several philosophical systems before his conversion, and after it, in the philosopher's dress, he preached the word of God.[1] The account which he gives us of his studies in philosophy, and his subsequent conversion, is very interesting and instructive. To be led and to be approved by God, seems to have been the object of all his studies, and, knowing no better guide, he chose philosophy. It was the duty, he thought, of philosophy to investigate the Deity, and with this notion he tried the different schools in turn.[2] First he put himself under the instruction of a Stoic.[3] When he had spent a considerable time with him, he was disappointed at finding that he had gained no certain knowledge of God. His master told him that he himself knew nothing of the subject, and that indeed such knowledge was unnecessary. Leaving him in consequence, Justin went to a Peripatetic, a man who was a shrewd teacher in his own estimation. He, after a few days, asked for a fee, that their intercourse might not be without profit. This very unphilosophic request disgusted Justin, and he at once sought for another teacher. Still eager, he went to a Pythagorean, a very celebrated man, who prided himself greatly on his wisdom. But when Justin applied for admission to the number of his hearers and disciples, he was asked, "Are you acquainted with music, astronomy, and geometry? Do you expect to comprehend those things which conduce to a happy life, without being first informed on those

---

[1] Eus. Hist. Ecc. iv. 11.   [2] Dialogue, c. 1.
[3] Ib. c. 2.

points, which wean the soul from objects of sense to the contemplation of intellectual objects, so that it may be able to discern the things which are essentially honourable and good?" Dismissal followed a confession of ignorance, and Justin was much cast down, for he had a high opinion of this teacher, and thought it would be far too tedious a business to acquire a knowledge of these necessary preliminaries. Lastly, he tried a Platonist sage. With him he improved and made rapid advance daily, and the Platonic conception of immaterial things captivated him, and its theory of ideas furnished his mind with wings, so that in a little time he supposed that he had become wise, and, such was his folly, hoped shortly to see God—the end of Plato's philosophy. Whilst thus disposed, wishing to be quiet and alone, he was one day walking in a field by the seaside; an old man by no means contemptible in appearance, but of venerable and meek manners, followed him at a little distance. The following conversation followed:—

Old Man. Why are you here?

Justin. I delight in such walks, because my attention is not distracted; such places are most fit for the study of philology.

O. M. Are you, then, a philologian (*i.e.* a lover of words), but no lover of deeds or of truth?

J. What greater work could one accomplish than to show the reason which governs all; and having laid hold of it, and being supported by it, to look down on the errors of others.[1] Without philosophy

---

[1] Notice the pride of the philosopher here.

and right reason none would possess prudence. Therefore it is necessary to philosophize, and account it the greatest and most precious of gains, all other things being reckoned in comparison of second or third-rate importance.

O. M. Does philosophy, then, confer happiness?

J. Assuredly; and it alone.

O. M. What, then, is philosophy? and what is happiness?

J. Philosophy is the knowledge of that which is, and the discernment of the truth; and happiness is the reward of this knowledge of wisdom.

O. M. What do you define God to be?

J. That which is ever one and the same, and the cause of being to all other creatures,—that is God.

The old man is pleased at this answer, and asks,— "Is not knowledge a term common to different things? For whoever is skilled in any of the arts is said to have knowledge of it. But this cannot be said equally well of divine and human things. Is there any science, for instance, which gives us the knowledge of things divine and human, and likewise of the divinity and righteousness in them?"

J. Certainly there is.

O. M. What! can we know God and man in the same way as we may know music, arithmetic, astronomy, and the like?

J. By no means.

O. M. Of some things we have knowledge by study or application, of others by sight. If any were to tell you that an animal exists in India of a nature unlike all others, you would not know it before you saw it, or until you had heard from one who had seen it?

J. Certainly not.

Now comes the crucial question. He wants to show Justin that philosophy cannot give knowledge of God, or, according to Justin's own definition, " *That which is.*" Philosophers cannot know that which they have not seen, so he asks,—

" How, then, do philosophers know God, or speak the truth about Him, when they have neither seen Him at any time, nor heard Him? "

J. God is not to be discerned by the eyes, but by the mind, so Plato teaches, and so I believe.

Now the object of the old man is to show that God cannot be discerned by the unassisted mind, so he asks,—

" How is it that the mind can see God? "

J. From its nature, and relationship to God.

Then the old man's object is to show that it is not natural to man to comprehend God, *i.e.*, that man cannot by searching find out God. So he drives Justin to admit that the comprehension of God is not a characteristic common to all minds; some have it, and some have it not. He makes him confess that the philosophers cannot tell him what the soul of man really is. He convinces him that the soul has nothing which it has not received, and at last induces Justin to ask, " Whom, then, shall a man take as his master? or whence shall he derive any instruction if the truth is not with these philosophers? " And now the old man has got to the point he wished. In order to attain to the knowledge of God, man wants a Divine teacher. He cannot see God with his eyes, as Justin allows. He cannot naturally comprehend God with his mind, as he has been compelled to admit; but God reveals Himself to men, and in this way :—

"There once lived men," the old man says, "called prophets, who were anterior to any of those who are considered philosophers, both righteous and beloved by God. These spoke by the Holy Ghost, and foretold what would happen hereafter, and what is now taking place. These alone knew and taught the truth, neither regarding nor fearing any man, nor being themselves carried away by the love of glory, but declaring those things alone which they saw and heard, when filled with the Holy Ghost. Their writings are still extant, and he who has read them will derive much instruction about the first principles and the ends of things, together with all those matters that a philosopher ought to know after he has believed them. They have not indeed given demonstrations in their writings, for they, in fact, as faithful witnesses of the truth, are above all demonstration; but the events which have happened already, and those which are taking place even now, compel you to receive their testimony. Even, indeed, for the miracles which they performed are they worthy of belief, and especially since they glorified God the Father and Maker of all things, and taught concerning Christ His Son who was sent by Him, which the false prophets, who were filled with a spirit of falsehood and uncleanness, neither did nor do; but these presume to perform certain wonders to astonish mankind, and set forth the praises of lying spirits and devils. But do you, above all things, pray that the gates of light may be opened to you; for these things are not to be seen or comprehended, except by him to whom God and His Christ give the grace of understanding."

When the old man had said this and many other things, he went away, and Justin never saw him again. But straightway a fire was kindled in his soul, and a love of the prophets and the friends of Christ possessed him; and when he had considered the matter, he found the Christian philosophy alone safe and profitable. It became his desire and aim that others should become as he was. He endeavoured to persuade others to give credence to the Saviour's words, to become acquainted with the Christ of God, and, being initiated, lead a happy life.

We have described Justin's conversion at great length, because it describes so plainly the difference between philosophy and Christianity. On the one side there was human reasoning, on the other Divine revelation; on the one side there was demonstration of truth, on the other witnesses to truth; on the one side there was nature, on the other grace.

Probably, Justin would not have been thus easily converted, had not Christians by their deaths already recommended their doctrines to his mind. He had seen how Christians could die before he knew what Christianity was. He had already come to the conclusion that the popular slanders were utterly false. "I myself," he says, "when I was delighting in the doctrines of Plato, and heard the Christians slandered, and saw them fearless of death, and of all other things which are counted fearful, perceived that it was impossible they could be living in wickedness and pleasure." He laughed at the wicked disguise which evil spirits had thrown round the divine doctrines of the Christians, and then, being instructed by the old man, he strove with all his strength to become a Christian, and endeavoured in his turn to lead others to Christ. Of course, being thus eager in the Christian cause, he ran the greatest risks. He was quite aware of this. He tells us that he expected to be entrapped and affixed to the stake by some of his heathen opponents.[1] He mentions especially one Crescens, a Cynic philosopher, who was a lover of noise and boasting, a false and ignorant accuser of the brethren, in order to please the multitude. Justin had publicly refuted him in argument, and so incurred his hatred. These expectations were fulfilled; Crescens did bring about his martyrdom at Rome.[2] He was brought before the prefect Rusticus along with others. He refused to offer libations to vain idols. He confessed he was a Christian.[3] He was asked scoffingly whether he supposed that if he was scourged and beheaded, he would ascend into heaven, He answered that he did not suppose, but was fully persuaded of it. All threats were in vain. Sentence was pronounced. "Let those who have refused to do sacrifice to the gods and to yield to the comand of the Emperor, be scourged, and led away to suffer the punishment of decapitation, according to the laws." The holy martyrs then glorified God, and "went out to the

---

[1] Apol. ii. c. 3.   [2] Tatian, quoted by Eusebius, iv. 16.
[3] Martyrdom of Justin and others.

accustomed place.[1] They were beheaded, and perfected their testimony in the confession of the Saviour. Some of the faithful having secretly removed their bodies, laid them in a suitable place, the grace of our Lord Jesus Christ having wrought along with them to whom be glory for ever and ever, Amen."

Three undisputed works of Justin, all of them of an Apologetic character, are now extant; namely, the two Apologies and the Dialogue with Trypho. All of them contain remarkable passages, and all of them are deficient in order, and method, and logic. Much that is most valuable to us seems unsuitable for the object for which it was written. Of course, this latter fault was a very natural one to fall into, especially under the particular circumstances. To know the arguments which will influence men of principles wholly diverse from your own, is a rare gift in every age. And Justin was treading on wellnigh unknown ground. Later Apologists were able to use his materials, and, in some measure, to avoid his mistakes.

Justin's first Apology was addressed to the Emperor Antoninus Pius and his sons, the Sacred Senate, and the whole Roman people. He calls it a petition on behalf of those of all nations who are unjustly hated and wantonly abused, he himself being one. Rumour had spread certain charges against the Christians. He asks for an investigation. He appeals to the piety and philosophy of the rulers whom he addresses. They are guardians of justice and lovers of learning, and he demands justice at their hands. A mere

---

[1] Martyrdom of Justin and others, c. 5.

name proves nothing one way or another. The name Christian, so far as it goes, is an argument in favour of the people who bear it. "We are (by name) most excellent people. To hate what is excellent is unjust.[1] Granted that some called Christians have ere now been arrested and convicted as evil-doers,[2] you must not allow the evil deeds of some to discredit the character of all. Under the one name of philosopher are banded together many who do nothing worthy of their profession: many of diverse opinions and teachings; some who have even taught atheism. You discriminate between philosophers, you ought to discriminate between Christians. Remember, to our credit, that it is very easy for us to avoid your persecution; you condemn us for our mere name; you acquit us if we are willing to deny our name. Why is it that we refuse so to do? It is because we would not live by telling a lie."

The charges he mentions as brought against the Christians are Atheism and Immorality; there is also a reference to a Political charge. In answer to these he remarks, that although atheists with respect to the demon-gods of the heathen, the Christians have a God whom they serve. Him they worship, but not with sacrifices and libations, for they have been taught that God, the provider of all things, needs no material offerings at the hands of men, and that the service He accepts is the imitation of the excellences

---

[1] Chrestus is the Greek for "excellent," and Justin here makes use of that fact.

[2] The followers of Simon Magus (c. 26), and probably also the Gnostics generally, are alluded to here.

which dwell in Him. Him they serve, because they desire to live with Him in His kingdom, because they fear everlasting fire. And as this system of rewards and punishments is divine, and therefore perfect, it necessarily has a much greater influence on their conduct than any human and imperfect system. How can they lead wicked lives when they know they cannot escape punishment? It is quite true the Christians look for a kingdom, but the kingdom is not human, it is with God. If it were human, they would deny Christ in order that they might not be slain; for death would cut them off from the fulfilment of their hopes.

He then gives the source of Christian teaching. Their doctrine has been taught them by the Word of God, Jesus Christ, who was born for this purpose, and was crucified under Pontius Pilate, procurator of Judæa in the times of Tiberius Cæsar.

In forcible language Justin describes the change which this doctrine has wrought on the lives of those who have received it. "Since our persuasion by the Word," he says, "we stand aloof from the demons, and follow the only unbegotten God through His Son; we, who formerly delighted in fornication, now embrace chastity alone; we, who formerly used magical arts, dedicate ourselves to the good and unbegotten God; we, who valued above all things the acquisition of wealth and possessions, now turn what we have into a common stock, and communicate to every one in need; we, who hated and destroyed one another, and would not even use the same hearth or fire with the men of a different tribe, on account of their different manners, now, since the coming of Christ, live familiarly with them, and pray for our enemies, and endeavour to persuade those who hate us unjustly to live conformably to the good precepts of Christ, to the end that they may become partakers with us of the same joyful hope of a reward from God."

Lest Justin should appear to be reasoning sophistically, he gives at great length the teaching of Christ on matters of life and conduct. He shows how Christ taught His disciples to be chaste even in thought, to love even their enemies, to lay up treasure in heaven and not on earth, to be patient under injuries, to swear not at all. His system is such a practical one, that it is not believing a certain set of opinions, but acting them out in the life, which constitutes a Christian. He taught them to render to Cæsar the things that are Cæsar's, so that they are necessarily obedient subjects. All these precepts the Christians are duly carrying out, and if any break them, then they cease, *ipso facto*, to be Christians, and will be deservedly punished.

He then endeavours to show that the Christian doctrines of the Immortality of the Soul, the Resurrection of the Body, and the Incarnation of the Deity, are not, *à priori*, incredible to a heathen, for his own mythology contains similar doctrines. The arguments he adduces here seem to be of a very doubtful and fanciful character.

The Analogy of Nature furnishes him with an additional argument in favour of the Resurrection. He asks whether it is more difficult to believe that the body of a man sown in the earth should, in God's appointed time, rise again and put on incorruption, or to believe that from a small drop of seed, bones, and sinews, and flesh should be formed in human shape. We should not have believed the latter, had not experience convinced us. We have no right to deny the possibility of the former, though hitherto beyond our experience.

Justin now states the three points which he wishes to prove.

(1.) That the Christian doctrine is alone true, and that it is to be received, not because of its resemblance to heathen doctrine, but on its own authority.

(2.) That Jesus Christ is the only Son of God—being His Word, and First Begotten, and Power.

(3.) That the demons have enabled the poets and others to anticipate the facts of His life.

To prove the first point (c. 24–29), Justin remarks that the heathen themselves are at variance as to the proper objects of worship. Some of them worship lifeless objects, some irrational animals; the things which some esteem gods, others esteem wild beasts. If any one goes back to their ancient mythology, he finds their gods perpetrating crimes too base for men to mention: those cannot be gods who are slaves to human passions. To come later down, the heathen have esteemed even magicians worthy of divine honours. The practical result of these doctrines is, that they expose their children, or rear them for shameful uses; that immorality and unnatural crimes are legalized, and that crimes are perpetrated under the title of religious mysteries. Surely, a religion so uncertain in its objects of worship, whose gods are so despicable either from their vices or from their weakness, whose votaries lead such immoral lives, cannot but be false. Him whom the heathen esteem a god, the Christians call the devil, who will hereafter be sent, along with his worshippers, to eternal punishment. This punishment has been delayed simply because of God's regard for the human race. The Christians, on the other hand, live continently; they worship a God who delights in virtue, who made the human race with the power of thought, and choosing the truth, and doing what is right.

To prove the second point (c. 30–53), Justin meets, at the outset, the objection that Christ worked His wonderful works by magical art, and thus appeared, to be the Son of God. The Christ of prophecy can have been no magician. The books which tell of Him are no cunningly devised fables, framed after the event; they were translated for a heathen king hundreds of years before He of whom they spoke appeared upon earth. They do not exist in rare copies, but are in the possession of all Jews throughout the world. They are not the longings of one mind and one age, but in the succession of generations during 5,000 years, prophets after prophets arose. They are no ambiguous oracles, giving doubtful and shadowy information, but they tell of his age, nation, tribe, miraculous conception, place of birth, miraculous powers, character, and death, together with numerous circumstances of His life. It is not isolated expressions, on which coincidences might be hung, which point to Him, but whole chapters together. No man before Him has ever realized the predictions, for they foreshadow one who should be more than man. It must not, however, be supposed that "whatever happens, happens by a fatal necessity, because it is foretold as known beforehand." The balancings of a man between good and evil, and the very existence of good and evil, prove this. The same Spirit which foretold future events thus taught, —"Behold, before thy face are good and evil; choose the good." It was not to be believed that men who lived before the birth of Christ were left without instruction. The coming Word cast its light before it, and shone on all races of men, as well on barbarian as on Greek, on Socrates as on Abraham.

As independent evidence of the fulfilment of prophecy, Justin adduces the case of the Jews. The desolation of Jerusalem was prophesied, and this very day guards are set, that no one may dwell there. All prophecy is not as yet fulfilled, but the past fulfilments are an earnest of the future, the First Advent is an earnest of the Second. It was not to the Jews alone that Christ came. He was no local national deliverer, but one whom the prophets declare will have more followers among the Gentiles than among the Jews.

To prove the third point (c. 54–64), Justin brings forward the legend of Bacchus, the horse of Bellerophon, the strength of Hercules, the miracles of Æsculapius, and the works of Plato, in which he sees manifest plagiarisms from the sacred writers. One thing, however, the demons did not understand,

and that was the Crucifixion; and yet the form of the cross lies at the basis of all things in the world.

He traces the sign of the cross in the sail of a ship, in the plough, in the tools of diggers and mechanics, and in the human form. "The human form," he says, "differs from that of the irrational animals in nothing else than in its being erect and having the hands extended, and having on the face extending from the forehead what is called the nose, through which there is respiration for the living creature; and this shows no other form than that of the cross." The power of the cross he tells the heathen, is shown by their own symbols on the banners and trophies; in their state processions they use it unwittingly as the insignia of their power and government. With this form they consecrate the images of their emperors when they die. After these remarks, which it is difficult to take seriously, Justin thinks he has proved this part of his case so well, that he is blameless if men still disbelieve.

The demons were not satisfied with anticipating the facts of the Incarnation; after Christ's appearance they put forth men like Simon Magus, who did mighty works by means of magic, and deceived many. It is they who cause persecution. It is they who put forward heretics like Marcion, who denied that God is the creator of heaven and earth.

As the Christian assemblies had been asserted to be immoral, Justin then gives a simple account of their meetings for worship and the administration of their sacraments; and he concludes by appealing to the Emperor to act as his father Hadrian had done, and to do this, not on the ground of Hadrian's decision, but on the ground of justice.

It may not be amiss to add here the decree of Hadrian referred to. It is quoted by Eusebius in his 'Ecclesiastical History,' and is undoubtedly genuine. It throws considerable light on the relations of the common people to the Christians.

Hadrian's Epistle to Minucius Fundanus, Proconsul of Asia, circa 124.

"I have received an epistle written to me by the most illustrious Serenius Granianus, whom you have succeeded. I do not wish that his communication should be passed over without examination, lest men should be disturbed, and occasion be given to informers for practising villainy. Accordingly if the people of your province will so far sustain this petition of theirs as to accuse the Christians in some court of law, they may pursue this course, but they are not to proceed by mere petitions and outcries. It is far more seemly, if any one should wish to make an accusation, that you should examine it. If, therefore, any one makes an accusation and proves these men to be acting contrary to the laws, decide the case according to the heinousness of the offence. But if any one, by Hercules, should put forward an accusation for mere calumny's sake, investigate the case according to its criminality, and take care that you inflict due punishment."[1]

Justin's Apology is said to have elicited an epistle

[1] Eus. Hist. Ecc. iv. 9.

of the Emperor Antoninus Pius to the Common Assembly of Asia.[1] Its authenticity is doubtful, for the Emperor contrasts disadvantageously the heathen with the Christians. The heathen neglect the worship of God, and persecute those who do serve Him. The Christians are to be unmolested, unless they attempt anything against the Roman Government; they are not to be punished simply on the ground of their religion. Whether this epistle is genuine or not, it is certain Antoninus Pius issued some decrees in favour of the Christians. Melitœ, in the fragment of his Apology (A.D. 170) preserved by Eusebius, distinctly states this.[2]

Passing over Justin's second Apology as not requiring separate attention, we come next to his Dialogue with Trypho. It differs fundamentally in character from the other Apologies; it is a defence of Christianity against the Jews, and it is based upon the prophecies of the Old Testament. It does not aim at proving that the Christians are worthy of toleration, but that Jesus is the Messiah, and that the Mosaic Law is abrogated.

In the introductory part of the work, we[3] have that interesting account of Justin's studies previous to his becoming a Christian, and of the circumstances of his conversion, already quoted at length. [4] In the actual argument, Trypho admits the groundlessness of the charges of immorality brought against the Christians, and confesses the wonderful character of the precepts of the Gospel; so wonderful, indeed,

[1] Eus. H. E. iv. 13. [2] Ib. iv. 26.
[3] Just. Dial. c. 2–8. [4] c. 10.

are these, that he suspects no man can keep them. The objections that he brings against the Christians[1] are, that, although they profess to be so pious, they observe no festivals or sabbaths, they do not practise the rite of circumcision, and they rest their hopes on a man who was crucified.

Justin's argument[2] in reply is,—that the Mosaic Law is now abrogated; that a new covenant has been made, as the prophets foretold; that righteousness does not consist in observing the Jewish rites, but in the circumcision of the foreskin of the heart, the baptism of the soul, the fast from sin, the purging oneself from the deeds of the old leaven. He considers[3] that the Mosaic laws were instituted only because of the weakness and wickedness of the Jewish nation. Circumcision was a sign of separation from the rest of the world, that so God's punishments might be inflicted on the Jews, and on them alone. They were enjoined to offer sacrifices to God, in order that they might not offer them to idols. They were commanded to abstain from certain meats, lest they should wax fat and kick. Sabbaths were instituted, because of their unrighteousness and the unrighteousness of their fathers. That the Jewish rites were not necessary to salvation, is proved by the fact, that they were not enjoined on any from Adam to Moses, and never on any but the Jews themselves. His remarks show plainly enough, that in his days no one had conceived the notion of what is now called the Christian sabbath. He speaks of circumcision, sabbaths, and feasts, as alike enjoined,

---

[1] c. 10.   [2] c. 11–24.   [3] c. 19–22.

because of the hardness of the hearts of the Jews, and as alike done away with in the new covenant. When Trypho quotes against him the well-known passage in Isaiah, lxviii. 13, 14, concerning the sabbath, he replies, that the observance was re-enjoined by the prophets for the same reason that it had originally been enjoined by Moses.

The remainder of the Dialogue is mainly taken up with Justin's proofs,—

(1.) That Jesus is the Christ.

(2.) That Christ is God.

He rests his arguments entirely upon the prophecies of the Old Testament.

It is difficult for any one with Western modes of thought to estimate the force with which Justin's arguments would fall upon one of his own race or time. His arguments rarely appear complete. There is always something wanting in the connection,—at least to a matter-of-fact Western mind. Resemblances, analogies, and direct prophecies seem with him to have an equal cogency. He sees and expects Trypho, an unbelieving Jew, to see in the two goats of the day of Atonement, the two Advents of Christ; in the twelve bells of the high priest, the twelve apostles; and in the Theophanies to Abraham, the doctrine of the Trinity. The wood of the cross is clearly symbolized by the rod of Moses; the tree cast into the waters of Marah, the rod which Jacob put into the water-troughs; Aaron's rod which budded, "the rod and the staff" of which David speaks in the twenty-third Psalm, and in the stick which Elisha cast into the Jordan, that the iron might swim. Leah and Rachel represented the Jews and Gentiles; for both of them, Christ, typified by Jacob, became a servant. The speckled and many-spotted sheep, Jacob's allotted hire, were the various and many-formed races of mankind which Christ purchased by His blood. Leah was weak-eyed, and the eyes of the souls of the Jews were excessively weak. Rachel stole Laban's gods, and. has hid them to this day, and the Christians have lost their ancestral gods of wood and stone. Justin, in dealing with the prophecies of the Old Testament, seems to start with the assumption that every sentence may be severed from its context, and interpreted according to pleasure; that any allusion or coincidence thus obtained to the life, teaching, or nature of Jesus, proves either the passage to be a prophecy, or Jesus to be the Christ. It is hardly to be wondered at that he thus failed in dealing with the evidence of prophecy. The subject was in itself exceedingly difficult. No sound rules for his guidance had been laid down; he does not seem to have had any special qualifications for his task; his judgment seems to have been faulty, and his imagination excessive.

The death upon the cross was the great stumbling-block to Trypho.[1] He made no great difficulty in admitting the doctrine of a suffering Messiah, but he could not believe that He would be shamefully crucified.[2] It is impossible to suppose that his difficulties would in any way be removed by Justin's enumeration of those passages of the Old Testament in which he thought the cross was typified,—doubtful allusions,

---

[1] Just. Dial. c. 89. [2] c. 90.

at the very best, they could have no argumentative force to an unbeliever.[1] When confronted by the text, "Cursed is every one that hangeth on a tree," Justin replies very differently to some in the present day.[2] He allows that Christ was cursed, not, however, by God, but by the Jews, who cursed both Him and those that believed on Him.

As a defence of Christianity against the Jews, Justin's Dialogue with Trypho is of little value to us. Its chief value consists in the view it gives of the principles of interpretation prevalent at the time, and in the testimony it gives that the story of Christ's life, then current, was substantially the same as that contained in the Gospels. It is obvious that a work like this has very little in common with the other Apologies.

TATIAN. CIRCA 150 A.D.

There is something melancholy in considering Tatian's address to the Greeks; for this defender of the faith ultimately made shipwreck of his own, and founded an heretical sect. He rejected marriage as impure, and refused the meats which God created to be received with thanksgiving. His heresy appears to have been similar to that condemned by St. Paul in his Epistle to the Colossians. "Touch not, taste not, handle not," would seem to have been one of his principles. He is said to have composed a harmony of the four Gospels, and to have left out all the parts that related to the Incarnation and the true manhood of Christ.

[1] c. 91–97.   [2] c. 94–96.

THE GREEK APOLOGISTS. 151

Tatian writes as a barbarian to Greeks, and he scoffs at the Greek pride, and the Greek philosophy, and the Greek religion. He had been a great proficient in their wisdom, and had been admitted to their mysteries. He had examined their religious rites, and found they sanctioned wickedness. Disgusted with all, he retired by himself to discover the truth; and, he says, "While I was giving my most earnest attention to the matter, I happened to meet with certain Barbaric writings, too old to be compared with the opinions of the Greeks, and too divine to be compared with their errors; and I was led to put faith in these by the unpretending cast of the language, inartificial character of the writers, the foreknowledge displayed of future events, the excellent quality of the precepts, and the declaration of the government of the universe as centred in one Being; and my soul being taught of God, I discerned that the former (Greek philosophy) set of writings leads to condemnation, but that these put an end to the slavery that is in the world, and rescue us from a multiplicity of rulers and ten thousand tyrants; while they give us, not indeed what we had not before received, but what we had received, but were prevented by error from retaining (c. 30). Therefore, being initiated and instructed in these things, I wish to put away my former errors as the follies of childhood."

The Greek religion is regarded by Tatian as demon-worship (c. 8, 10). The demons have reduced men to slavery, and perverted their minds from heavenly things by a deceptive display of power; they are the examples of all crime (c. 16, 17). The depravity of man is the secret of their strength, for they minister to men's lusts (c. 17, 19). He rejects the Greek philosophy on account of its arrogant, unpractical, and indefinite nature (c. 2, 3), and because of the vices, errors, and quarrels of the philosophers. He speaks bitterly throughout (c. 25, 27). His Christianity had not made him a happy man (c. 32). The shadow of his apostasy seems to be cast before. Gnostic tendencies can be traced in his Apology (c. 12, 13, 15, 16); but inasmuch as he believed that the world was created by the Word (c. 5), that the body would rise again (c. 6), and that no distinction was to be made between Christians (c. 32), it cannot be said that these tendencies had attained as yet a high degree of development.

ATHENAGORAS. DATE OF APOLOGY, 177 A.D.

Athenagoras next claims our attention. He, like Justin, when he became a Christian, did not cease to be a philosopher. He styles himself Christian and philosopher, in the title of his Apology. If we may believe a tradition of the 5th century, he was converted to Christianity whilst presiding over the Academic School at Alexandria.[1] It was his object, like Celsus, to write against the Christians. For this purpose he studied the Divine Scriptures, and while thus engaged, he was himself caught by the All-Holy

---

[1] So Philip of Side. See Art. "Athenagoras," Smith's Dictionary of Christian Biography.

Spirit, so that, like Paul, he became a teacher of the faith which once he persecuted. He addressed his "Embassy" for the Christians, about the year 177 A.D., "to the Emperors Marcus Aurelius and Commodus, conquerors of Armenia and Sarmatia; and more than all, philosophers." His opening words are remarkable, and show the grounds on which he claimed toleration.

"In your empire," he says, "greatest of sovereigns, different nations have different customs and laws; and no one is hindered by law or fear of punishment from following his ancestral usages, however ridiculous these may be. A citizen of Ilium calls Hector a god, and pays divine honours to Helen, taking her for Adrasteia. The Lacedæmonian venerates Agamemnon as Zeus, and Phylonoë the daughter of Tyndarus, and the men of Tenedos worship Tennes. The Athenian sacrifices to Erectheus as Poseidon. The Athenians also perform religious rites and celebrate mysteries in honour of Agraulus and Pandrosus, women who were deemed guilty of impiety for opening the box. In short, among every nation and people, men offer whatever sacrifices, and celebrate whatever mysteries, they please. The Egyptians reckon among their gods, even cats, and crocodiles, and serpents, and asps, and dogs. And to all these, both you and the laws give permission so to act; deeming, on the one hand, that belief in no god at all is impious and wicked; and on the other, that it is necessary for each man to worship the gods he prefers, in order that through the fear of the deity, man may be kept from wrong-doing."

Why, he goes on to ask, is a mere name odious to you? Names are not deserving of hatred; it is the unjust act that calls for punishment. Throughout the empire all enjoy equal rights and profound peace; all, except the Christians. Not that they had committed any wrong. Nay! as he will show, they are of all men most piously and righteously disposed toward God and the rulers of the State, and yet it was allowed to the multitude to harass, plunder, and persecute them simply for their name. He ventures to lay a statement of their case before the emperors. If any can convict them of a crime, be it great or small, they do not ask to be excused from judgment (c. 2); but if the accusations relate only to the name, if they rest only on popular talk, then it behoves the emperors to take legal measures for the removal of this despiteful treatment. Three charges, he says, were brought against the Christians, Atheism, Thyestean Feasts, Ædipodean intercourse (c. 3). If they are true, destroy us, root and branch, with our wives and children. If they are only idle tales and empty slanders, you ought to make inquiries concerning our life, our opinions, and our loyalty, and grant us the same rights as our persecutors.

Athenagoras then proceeds to defend the Christians on the three charges. The Christians were not atheists; they worshipped *one* God, and there could not be more than *one*. They did not worship images, for they distinguished God from material substances. They did not worship nature, they reckoned it to be only God's house, and they looked beyond to Him who made it. They did not worship the gods of the heathen, for they were but of yesterday, they had bodily form and fleshly desires. Poets and philosophers agreed with Christians here. It was the evil spirits, greedy of sacrificial odours and the blood of victims, who had seduced the ignorant to worship gods like these.

The stories of impious feasts had, he says, been made up, to justify the popular hatred, to terrify the Christians themselves, and to induce the ruler to deal harshly with them. He remarks that it has always been common for vice to make war on virtue. But the emperors, who excel in intelligence, must know, that that life which is directed towards God as its rule, is likely to be the most pure. The Christians' account is not with human laws, which a bad man can evade. They know that they are liable to God for the looks of their eyes, and the very thoughts of their hearts. Oh, what a difference there is between them and the heathen, with their impurities, and unnatural crimes, and their gladiatorial contests! The accusations brought are an example of the proverb, "The harlot reproves the chaste." The Christians will not even look upon murders in the games, how, then, is it likely that they will themselves commit murder? They believe in the resurrection of the dead, how is likely that they should make themselves tombs for bodies that will rise again? He concludes with the following appeal:—

"And now do you, who are entirely in everything, by nature and by education, upright, and moderate, and benevolent, and worthy of your rule, now that I have disposed of the several accusations, and proved that we are pious, and gentle, and temperate in spirit, bend your royal head in approval; for who are more deserving to obtain the things that they ask, than those who, like us, pray for your government, that you may, as is most equitable, receive the kingdom, son from father, and that your empire may receive increase and addition, all men becoming subject to your sway? And this is also for our advantage, that we may lead a peaceable and quiet life, and may ourselves readily perform all that is commanded us."

The "Embassy" of Athenagoras is a model apology. Its author had a clear conception of the arguments likely to attain his end; he knew how far to go, and when to stop. There was no danger in attacking the heathen religion and mythology in a work addressed to a philosopher like Marcus Aurelius; philosophers before him had done the same thing. Athenagoras studiously endeavours to place the Christians on the same footing with them; he uses their writings to show the reasonableness of Christian doctrine, and he is very sparing in his censure of them. On the other hand, he does not enter into minute discussion of Christian doctrines, or detailed accounts of Christian ceremonies, like Justin. He was simply endeavouring to deliver the Christians from persecution by clearing them from the charge of impiety and immorality, and all his statements have reference to this. His object is, to show that the Christian religion is at least as worthy of toleration as many others which the State tolerated without difficulty. The moderation, and elegance, and judgment, with which he states his case, are worthy of all praise.

EPISTLE TO DIOGNETUS. 120 A.D. CIRCA.

The Epistle to Diognetus is a very interesting anonymous fragment. Its first chapter gives us some of the points in Christian life and character which specially attracted the attention of the heathen, and led them to be curious about the Christians' God and the Christian religion.

Diognetus had observed that the Christians looked down upon the world, and despised death. He had noticed that they neither reverenced the Greek gods, nor held to the Jewish religion. He saw also that they cherished a remarkable affection amongst themselves. In consequence he inquired very earnestly and carefully in what God they trusted, and what religion they observed, and why it had been so late in entering into the world. The author cordially welcomes this desire, and prays God that he may speak to edification.

The author realizes very vividly the wretched state of the world before the coming of the Word. The heathen were worshipping images of wood and stone. The Jews were worshipping the true God in a wrong way. The doctrines of those philosophers deemed trustworthy, were vain and silly. God appeared to neglect men, and to have no care for them. He permitted them to be borne along by unruly impulses. Then, when it was manifest that we in ourselves were unable to enter into the kingdom of God, when our wickedness had reached its height, and punishment and death were impending over us—the one love of God did not remember our iniquity against us, but showed great long-suffering and bore with us. "He Himself took on Him the burden of our iniquities, He gave His own Son as a ransom for us, the Holy One for transgressors, the Blameless One for the wicked, the Righteous One for the unrighteous, the Incorruptible One for the corruptible, the Immortal One for them that are mortal. For what other thing was capable of covering our sins than His righteousness? By what other one was it possible that we, the wicked and ungodly, could be justified than by the only Son of God? O sweet exchange! O unsearchable operation! O benefits surpassing all expectation! that the wickedness of many should be hid in a single Righteous One, and that the righteousness of One should justify many transgressors. Having, therefore, convinced us in the former time that our nature was unable to attain to life, and having now revealed the Saviour, who is able to save even those things which it was impossible to save,—by both these facts God desired to lead us to trust in His kindness, to esteem Him our Nourisher, Father, Teacher, Counsellor, Healer, our Wisdom, Light, Honour, Glory, Power, and Life, so that we should not be anxious about food or clothing."

We do not often meet with passages like this in the Apologies. In fact, this letter is rather an exhortation than an apology. It makes no allusion to the charges brought against the Christian.

THEOPHILUS,
BISHOP OF ANTIOCH. 168–181 OR 186 A.D.

The three letters of Theophilus, Bishop of Antioch, to Autolycus, a heathen, may be passed over with a very slight notice. We know little of Theophilus himself; but it is worth noticing that he, too, owed his conversion to the reading of the Scriptures. He met with the writings of the prophets, and studied the prophecies, and believed (i. 14). Perhaps it is in consequence of this that he gives, in great detail, the Old Testament history, and lays great stress on the accurate and ancient information therein contained. His object seems to be to induce Autolycus to enter upon the same study (ii. 4–8). He contrasts the discordant and foolish statements of the poets and philosophers with the consistent, and harmonious, and God-inspired utterances of the long line of Hebrew prophets (ii. 9). Along with these he classes the Greek Sibyl, and he quotes from her at length an exhortation to forsake the worship of images, and to worship the one Supreme God, the Maker of heaven and earth (ii. 36). He rebuts the usual accusations in the usual way.

CLEMENT OF ALEXANDRIA, TEACHER OF THE CATECHETICAL SCHOOL AT ALEXANDRIA. 190–200 A.D.

Clement of Alexandria's address to the Greeks is quite as much hortatory as apologetic. He attacks the heathen religion, but does not defend the Christians from accusation. He endeavours to attract to Christianity by a description of the beauty of its doctrines. The spirit of the whole work is best illustrated by its opening chapter.

In the Greek legends certain minstrels were renowned for the power of their song. Amphion of Thebes had allured fishes, Arion of Methymna had surrounded Thebes with walls, by the power of music. The Thracian Orpheus had tamed wild beasts and transplanted trees, by the might of his song. "Do you believe," says Clement, "all these vain fables, and are you only incredulous concerning the Truth? Let us bring down from heaven, Truth, with Wisdom in all her brightness, and the sacred prophetic choir. Let her cast her rays all round on those sitting in darkness. Let all men cease to listen to their old, deceiving, demon-inspired hymns, and listen to the new, and immortal, and divine songs. Those minstrels were all deceivers, unworthy of the name, by their songs and incantations corrupting human life under the pretence of poetry, possessed with a spirit of sorcery for the purposes of destruction, celebrating crime, enticing to idols, bringing into bondage the free citizens of heaven. Not such is my song. It has come to loose, and that speedily, the bitter bondage of the tyrant demons, and to lead us back to the mild and loving yoke of piety; it recalls to heaven those who have been cast prostrate to the earth. It alone has tamed men, the most intractable of animals. Men were like the beasts, nay, were like the stocks and stones in their stupidity, like the serpents in their deceitfulness, like the wolves in their rapacity. But all such most savage beasts, and all such blocks of stone, the heavenly song has transformed into tractable men. Behold the might of the new song! It has made men out of stones, men out of beasts. The dead, even, have heard it, and have become partakers of the true life. The universe has been composed by it into melodious order, the discord of the elements has been tuned, so that the whole world has become harmony. This deathless strain has reached from pole to pole, and has harmonized all things according to the paternal counsel of God. On man himself, composed of body and soul, a microcosm, an instrument of many strings, tuned by the Holy Spirit, the Word of God makes melody. A beautiful breathing instrument of music the Lord made man. He is God's lute and harp, and to Him he sings accordant. The Celestial Word is also Himself the melodious holy instrument of God. He is the New Song, This instrument of God loves mankind. Many are the tones in in which He speaks to them. Sometimes He upbraids, sometimes He threatens, some men He mourns over, some men He cheers with His melody To all He speaks, and calls them to salvation, and rescues them from the wicked tyrant who binds them fast."

The whole exhortation is only an expansion of the ideas contained here. We have an exposure of the heathen mythology, the opinions of philosophers, and the fables of the poets. At the same time it is confessed that Plato and others touched the truth. The Scriptures (in which term he includes the Sibyl) alone present us with the appliances necessary for the attainment of piety. Devoid of outward beauty and embellishment, they raise up humanity strangled by wickedness, to despise the casualties of life. The prophets form one harmonious choir under one leader and teacher—The Word. They attain to and rest in the same truth, and cry, Abba, Father. Clement pictures the great blessings offered to the world by Christ. He describes Him as inviting all to come to Him. He urges all to hasten to accept the invitation.

It will thus be seen that this work of Clement, though commonly included amongst the Apologies, is really an exhortation to the heathen to become Christians. Its idea cannot be better expressed than in the words of a modern hymn :—

> Come, weary souls, for Jesus bids you come :
>   And through the dark, its echoes sweetly ringing,
> The music of the Gospel leads us home.

ORIGEN. 185–255 A.D.

Origen's life is far too vast a subject to deal with in a paragraph, and so we shall leave it untouched, and confine our attention to the Apology which he wrote. In one respect this is unique amongst early Apologies. It is not a general but a particular defence. It is an answer to a book written by a philosopher called Celsus, seventy years before. Origen's method is to take and refute *seriatim* the different accusations brought by him.

As we have already seen, Celsus was not a formidable antagonist. He knew many things about, but not much of, Christianity. He was well acquainted with the Gospel narrative, the Old Testament Scriptures, and the many legends which popular rumour, the malice of the Jews, and the unrestrained imagination of the heretics, had invented concerning Christians and their religion. But he had no notion of Christianity as a whole. He attacks particular points in it without considering them as parts of a system. He makes no consistent attack. His idea seems to be, that if he throws enough mud some of it will be sure to stick. He brings the ordinary accusations against the Christians, but with this difference, he endeavours to trace them home to the spirit of Christianity. Like others he charges them with *immorality* (iii. 59, 64, 73, 74), and this is natural enough, for the worst of men are invited to their society (i. 62, 63). He charges them with *foolishness*, and what are they always saying, but "Do not examine, but believe" (i. 9. 13). "The wisdom of this world is foolishness." He charges them with *impiety*, and, confounding them with the Gnostic heretics called Ophites, he declares it is part of their belief to execrate the Creator of the world.

Origen's defence necessarily took its form from the attack. He takes each statement of Celsus and investigates it separately. He clears away misrepresentations. He distinguishes between Catholics and Heretics, and he adduces the evidences of prophecy and miracles. Probably the extracts from Celsus are to us the most valuable part of Origen's work. There are extant many early Apologies for Christianity, but no complete early attack. It is important that we should be able to realize what appearance Christianity presented to the heathen of those early times, and this Origen's extracts effect for us in some measure.[1]

[1] See p. 120.

CHAPTER VIII.

THE LATIN APOLOGISTS.

We pass on to consider the Latin Apologists, who lived in the 3rd century A.D. We do not find them, as we might have expected, in the Church of Rome. In these early times she was distinguished rather for her zeal for the purity of the faith than for her learning. The African Church, now so utterly fallen to decay, gave to the Christians the earliest defenders who wrote in the Latin tongue.

TERTULLIAN. 150–220 A.D.

The first in time, and in other respects the most important of all the Latin Apologists, is Tertullian. Of his life we know little, but his works are most numerous and valuable, and leave untouched few points relating to Christian faith and practice. Amongst them are contained four treatises of an Apologetic nature. Two only need be considered by us, his "Apologetic Book," and his "Testimony of the Soul."

The Apology.—No early defence of the Christians can be compared in force and completeness with the "Apologetic Book" of Tertullian. We miss, indeed, that moderation, and elegance, and wide sympathy, which are found so markedly in the " Embassy " of Athenagoras. One cannot help feeling that Tertullian's logic was too keen for his purpose. He seems to wish to prove his case, rather than to win his cause. It was dangerous and impolitic to press home arguments, when the enemy had material power on his side. Retort was out of place in an Apology. It only embittered the controversy, and conciliation was required. Such considerations were, however, quite beneath Tertullian's notice. He seems to have been of a stern and harsh character. His own religion, and his judgment on that of others, were hard and unsympathizing. Hence we find him attacking the heathen with relentless vigour. His is not the tone of a suppliant pleading for toleration. He demands justice. Arraigned as a criminal at the bar, he accuses and condemns his judges.

His Apology was addressed to the governors and proconsulars of Africa, and was written almost exactly at the commencement of the third century. Like most of the Apologies, it is an appeal to the authorities that the Christians should not be condemned unheard. Tertullian opens his case by objecting to the mode of procedure at the trials. The forms of law were not observed. The accused were not allowed to defend themselves against the popular accusations. Their treatment was wholly different from that adopted at the trials of other criminals. When accused of the crime of Christianity, confession of guilt was followed by torture to force them to a denial of guilt. On the other hand, a denial of their guilt was at once accepted, and they were let go free. Inasmuch as, in the courts, all turned on the answer to the question, " Are you a Christian ?" it came to pass that the title Christian summed up in one word all the reproaches and accusations which the hatred of the times had invented. What is there in this name to excite your hatred? whether it be Christian, which speaks of anointing and Christ our founder, or Chrestian, as you wrongly call it, which tells of sweetness and benignity.

Proceeding from the trial to the accusation (c. 4), Tertullian is the first of the Apologists who goes fairly into the charge, that the Christians formed a body unrecognized by law.

When the Christians had been able to prove their innocence of the crimes charged against them, their accusers fell back on the authority of the laws, and said, "It is not *lawful* for you to exist." Tertullian argues that justice is the foundation of law. A thing should be unlawful, not because men wish it so to be, but because it ought so to be. This particular law has not dropped down from heaven ; if it is a bad one, it can be repealed. Laws have been changed, are being changed every day, and many still require to be changed ; then why not this, if reason be shown? He remarks that the laws against the Christians were only enforced by unjust and wicked emperors,—emperors like Nero, the first to assail them, and like Domitian, a man of the same type in cruelty; emperors like Trajan, Antoninus Pius, or Marcus Aurelius, had never persecuted them.[1] "What sort of laws," he

---

[1] Facts seem to be against Tertullian here.

asks, "are these which the impious only use against us? Moreover, who are you, that you should set yourselves up as protectors of the laws and institutions of your fathers? Where is the ancient simplicity of life, and purity of morals? It is utterly gone. What has become of your ancient religion? You have introduced new gods. In your dress, your food, your style of life, in your opinions, and even in your speech, you have renounced your ancestors.

Proceeding to the charges of *immorality*, Tertullian argues that they rest, notwithstanding watches and surprises, on rumour only. "Everybody knows what sort of a thing rumour is; it is essentially lying. Even its truths are mixed with falsehood; it is the very designation of uncertainty. It has no place when proof is given and the truth is known. Does any but a fool put his trust in it? Yet it is the only witness you can bring against us (c. 8). Moreover, these charges are intrinsically improbable. Human nature is incapable of such baseness. Christians are men as well as you." Then, curiously but characteristically enough, Tertullian turns round (c. 9), and retorts the same charges against the heathen; in so doing, he overthrows, of course, this last argument.

The *theological* charge next receives his attention (c. 10). "You do not," said the heathen, "worship the gods, and you do not offer sacrifice to the Emperor." His answer is, "No, we do not; for the gods you worship are no gods at all." To prove his point he examines the statements made concerning them in heathen books; he shows that they are not gods by nature, but originally men; that they were not made gods, either because the great God needed their aid, or wished to reward their merit (c. 11). The God who created and ordered the world in the beginning, needed no help from men for the governing of it. The merits of the heathen deities were not of a kind to have raised them to heaven, but rather to have sunk them into the lowest depths of hell. As for the images of the gods, in what do they differ from common vessels and utensils?

He draws an amusing parallel between the making of images and the persecuting of Christians. The heathen make gods in the same way that they kill Christians. "In their fashioning you fix them to frames, and in our execution you fix us to crosses and stakes; you tear our sides with claws, you use axes, and planes, and rasps on every member of their body. We are headless when you have done your worst upon us, they are headless before you have used your lead, and glue, and nails. You drive us to wild beasts, and lions and tigers are their constant attendants. We are burnt in the fire, and so is the metal of which they are composed. We are condemned to the mines, and from thence their original lump came. We are banished to islands,—in islands it is common for the gods to be born or to die. Spite of all this, 'They are gods to us,' you say (c. 12). Indeed! How is it, then, that you are convicted of impious and sacrilegious conduct to them? With you, deity depends upon a decision of the Senate. With you, gods are pledged, sold, broken up, changed into cooking-pots and firepans. With you, deity is made a gain of and farmed out to the highest bidder. The more sacred a god is, the larger is the tax he pays. Majesty is made a source of gain. Religion goes about the taverns begging. You enrol amongst your ancient gods your prostitutes, and sorcerers, and infamous court pages (c. 14). You offer as sacrifices diseased and dying animals (c. 15). You insult your objects of worship, in your books and theatres by your scoffs, in their temples and at their very altars by your crimes " (c. 16).

After denying the truth of certain absurd stories as to the object of the Christian worship, Tertullian describes what that object really is (c. 17). It is the one God, the Creator of all things, Invisible, Incomprehensible, the true God because immensely great. To Him His great and manifold works, and the simple soul of man bear witness (c. 18). Not these alone, His written Word also,—the writings of just men on whom He poured His Spirit; ancient writings, as the facts of history show (c. 19); true writings, as the fulfilment of prophecy proves (c. 20).

Up to this point, no Christian, as distinguished from Jewish, elements, have been introduced; but now Tertullian states the fundamental distinction between Judaism and Christianity (c. 21). The Jews consider Christ to be a mere man; the Christians believe Him to be God. He describes the nature of Christ's divinity. He is the Word of God, by whom all things were made. As the rays proceed forth from the sun, and there is no division, so the Son of God came forth from His Father, and yet the two are one. The Word was made flesh and dwelt amongst us, and proved His divinity by His wonderful works in His life, and His death, and His resurrection. Of these things Pilate was a witness, who sent an account of them to Tiberius.[1] Is there, then, anything in the origin and Founder of our Name that should cause you to persecute it so cruelly? Your duty is to search and see whether the divinity of Christ is true. If the acceptance of its truth transforms a man and makes him truly good, then you are bound (as we have felt ourselves already) to renounce the worship of other gods.

Tertullian now describes what the heathen worship really is. It is worship of demons. It is they who give to the heathen religion its power over men. They are the cause of all the mischief on the face of the world. Their great business is the ruin of mankind. Still, all unwillingly, they are most effective witnesses for Christ. When those possessed by them are brought to us, and we adjure them in the name of Christ, they confess what they are, even the gods you worship, and they bear testimony to the truth of Christian doctrine. Fearing Christ in God, and God in Christ, they become subject to the servants of God and Christ (c. 23). So at one touch and breathing, overwhelmed by the thought and realization of the judgment fires, they leave at our command the bodies they have entered, unwilling and distressed, and put to open shame (c. 24). The whole confession of these beings, in which they declare they are no gods, and that there is no God but one,—the God whom we adore, is quite sufficient to clear us from the crime of treason against the Roman religion. If these gods

[1] Tertullian is probably here referring to a Christian forgery.

have no existence, there is no religion in the case. Even if they have an existence, is it not generally held that there is One above them? Can we give His glory to another? Under any circumstances is unwilling homage of any value? All other nations, provinces, and even cities, have their own gods, why should we only be prevented from having a religion of our own?

The objection is now started, If the Christian theory is true, the heathen gods are no gods at all, and yet history shows that the Romans have been prosperous because they have been pious. Tertullian is treading on delicate ground now, and he is not the man to tread delicately (c. 25, 26). He proves, and proves conclusively, that history does not bear out this theory. The Romans were great before they were religious; they triumphed over gods, and not till then worshipped them. But he is not satisfied with this. He finds instances where the gods did not exercise their power in the defence of their worshippers, and he brings these forward as proofs of want of power. Non-exercise of Divine power, according to Tertullian, proves its non-existence. Every martyrdom showed the fallacy of this argument.

The last charge Tertullian meets is that of treason against the Emperor (c. 28). It was based simply on the fact that the Christians refused to pay him divine worship (c. 28-36). As Tertullian explains, the Christian religion forbids its followers to invoke a mere man—even the ruler of the world; but it requires them to invoke God for his safety, and to pay him the respect due to his position and to the minister of God (c. 32). They have special reasons for their prayers, for with the fall of the Roman empire will come the violent commotions which are impending over the whole world. As usual, Tertullian is not satisfied with showing that the Christians are loyal, but he proceeds to show that they alone are loyal (c. 35–36), he points to the prevalence of treason. In spite of the provocation the Christians have received, their names are not to be found in the lists of conspirators; their numbers make them formidable, but their principles make them harmless (c. 37).

Tertullian next explains (c. 38, 39) the nature of the Christian Society, with the intention of showing that it contains none of the characteristics of a faction, nothing to make it formidable to the State, and, therefore, nothing to prevent its toleration. He asserts (c. 40) that the Christians, so far from being the cause of public calamity, have been in reality the very salt of the earth. He meets and denies the charge of unprofitableness in the concerns of life (c. 42). He boasts of the superior morality of the Christians (c. 43, 44), and ascribes it to their rule of life, which is not human, but divine (c. 45).

And now we notice one of the characteristics of the Latin Apologists (c. 46): he is most anxious to maintain the independent claims of Christianity. Unbelief, convinced of the worth of Christianity, suggested that it was, notwithstanding, not really divine, but only a kind of philosophy. Innocence, justice, patience, sobriety, and chastity, were just the very things which the philosophers counselled and professed. "Is this so?" says Tertullian, "then why do you not treat us like the philosophers? No one compels a philosopher to sacrifice or take an oath. Nay, they openly overthrow your gods, and you applaud them for it. But are we, indeed, like the philosophers? Far from it. The name of philosophers drives out no wicked spirits; philosophers merely affect to hold the truth, and all the while they corrupt it. We Christians ardently and intensely long for it, and maintain it in its integrity. We are like philosophers neither in our knowledge nor in our ways. The philosophers do not know God; but He has been revealed to us. The philosophers do not practise the virtues they recommend: we must and do. No doubt the teachings of the philosophers and the Christians are, in some respects, similar (c. 47). The reason is, the poets and sophists have drunk from the fountain of the prophets. At least we are entitled to argue that our doctrines are not utterly foolish, if like to those of your wisest men (c. 49). The ideas, which in them are called sublime speculations and illustrious discoveries, cannot be called in us presumptuous speculations. If they are men of wisdom, we cannot be fools."

Tertullian concludes by appealing against the heathen cruelty (c. 50). The Christians glory in their sufferings, but they do not suffer willingly. They desire to suffer as the soldier longs for war. In suffering they reap glory and spoil, and in death they win the victory. The cruelty of the heathen is of no avail; the blood of the martyrs is the seed of the Church; the deeds of the Christians find more disciples than the words of the philosophers. No one who sees the fortitude of the Christians, fails to inquire what is the cause of it; no one who has inquired, fails to embrace their doctrines; no one who has embraced their doctrines, is unwilling to suffer for them, and thus obtain from God full forgiveness.

Tertullian's Apology is remarkable for its arrangement. He had a definite plan, and he always kept to it. He shows great discretion in the choice of his authorities. Elsewhere, he constantly quotes the Scriptures; here, very rarely. When he alludes to them, it is not to appeal to their authority but as containing information on Christian doctrine. Whatever its faults, the Apology of Tertullian holds the first place among the apologies of the age. It meets the accusations fully and completely, and so accomplishes its chief purpose. No one can fail to admire its earnest spirit. Although narrow and harsh in its judgments, it is the warm appeal of a warm heart.

The Testimony of the Soul.—We must not pass over, without notice, the argument against heathenism we find in Tertullian's treatise 'On the Testimony of the Soul.' He alone, of all the Apologists, refuses to search heathen literature for testimonies in favour of Christianity. Such arguments, he conceived, were easily set aside; they required great research for their acquisition, and a retentive memory for their use. So, in their place, he calls in a new witness, a witness more simple and better known—The soul of man; meaning thereby that part of man's nature which makes him a rational being in the highest degree capable of thought and knowledge. He will not have, indeed, the soul trained, and fashioned in, and corrupted by, the wisdom of the world, but the soul simple, rude, unlearned, untaught, as far as might be, except by itself and its Author. Not yet Christian, he presses it for a testimony on behalf of Christians. He draws this testimony from certain expressions which it uses naturally and constantly. When expressing its hopes and wishes, it does not invoke the *gods* for help, but it says, "Which may *God* grant," "If *God* so will." It thus acknowledges that there is *One* who is God and Sovereign. Yet again, it says, "God is good," and "God does good," and thus it declares the nature of God; and, by contrast, it seems to imply that man is evil, and has departed from God. It says, "God sees all; I commend thee to God:" "May God repay"; "God shall judge betwixt us"; and thus it confesses God's providence, His power, His justice, and a future retribution. It gives these testimonies whilst in the temples, and whilst engaged in the sacred rites. In the immediate presence of its gods, it appeals to the God who is elsewhere. And, besides, it gives a testimony to the immortality of the soul. When it speaks of the dead, it says, "Poor man." Why is a dead man poor, if he has lost the burden of life, and is beyond the feeling of pain? It curses the dead who have wronged it, and it blesses the dead to whom it is indebted for favours. It thus shows that they are not, in its idea, beyond the reach of blessing and curse. It says of one lately dead, "He is gone." He is expected to return, then. Nor can these testimonies be considered frivolous or feeble when it is recollected that the soul derives all its knowledge from Nature, and that Nature's teachings are derived from God. Is it a wonderful thing that, fallen though it is, it cannot forget its Creator, His goodness and His law, and its own end? Is it wonderful that, being divine in its origin, its revelation agrees with those made by God to His people in the Jewish Scriptures?

There is an obvious answer to this argument which Tertullian mentions. The expressions he has alleged may be only an accommodation to existing prejudices; they may have had their origin and become common from arguments used in books. To meet this, he appeals to the nature of language. A word is but an embodiment of a thought : thoughts are the offspring of the soul; words existed long before books; before the cultivated poet or philosopher came the rude and simple man. We have then to search for the origin of such expressions in the nature of man, who found need for them as expressing some deep feeling within him, or some truth which had been revealed to him from the beginning. If, indeed, the soul has taken them from writings at all, it must have done so from the earlier and not later ones, and the Scriptures of God are much more ancient than any secular literature.

And so Tertullian calls upon the heathen to give credence to the witness of the soul. He asks them to consider how it is it uses Christian phrases, though it hates Christians. From the whole wide world its testimony comes. "There is not a soul of man that does not," he says, "from the light that is in itself, proclaim the very things we are not permitted to speak above our breath. Most justly, then, every soul is a culprit as well as a witness. In the measure that it testifies for truth, the guilt of error lies on it. On the day of judgment it will stand before the courts of God without a word to say. Thou proclaimest God, O soul, but thou didst not seek to know Him. Evil spirits were detested by thee, and yet they were the objects of thy adoration; the punishments of hell were foreseen by thee, but no care was taken to avoid them; thou hadst a savour of Christianity, and withal wert the persecutor of Christians."

MINUCIUS FELIX. 200–250 A.D. CIRCA.

The Octavius of Minucius Felix is a lively and elegant Apology in the form of a dialogue between a Christian, Octavius (whence its name), and a heathen, Cœcilius. It is remarkable for giving a clear and complete picture of the Christians and their religion as they appeared in the eyes of the heathen world. In the introduction Minucius describes Octavius, then dead, as his most intimate friend. "He had been," he says, "my confidant in my love affairs, and my companion in my mistakes. When I emerged from the abyss of darkness into the light of wisdom and truth, he did not cast me off, but,—what is more glorious,—he outstripped me." The scene (so to speak) of the dialogue is laid as follows: On one occasion Octavius had come to Rome during the vacation time to visit

Minucius. Along with Cœcilius, a constant companion of the latter, they had gone to Ostia to take the mineral baths. Early one morning they were all walking together along the banks of the Tiber close to its mouth, and enjoying the gently-breathing air and soft yielding sand. Cœcilius perceived an image of the Egyptian god Serapis, and following the custom of the superstitious common people, he raised his hand to his mouth and kissed it. At once Octavius reproved Minucius for suffering his friend to remain in the darkness of idolatry. It was not the part of a good man so to do. The error of his friend was reflected upon himself. At the moment nothing more seems to have been said on the subject. They have now come to the sea-shore, and they walk along the beach. "There the gently rippling wave was smoothing the outside sands, as if it would level them for a promenade; and as the sea is always restless even when the winds are lulled, it came up on the shore, although not with waves crested and foaming, yet with waves crisped and curling. Just then we were excessively delighted at its vagaries, as on the very threshold of the water we were wetting the soles of our feet, and now the wave broke over them, and then retiring sucked itself to itself." As they walked along, Octavius beguiled the way with stories of navigation. On their return they came to a place where boats were lying on wooden slips, and they saw some boys eagerly gesticulating as they played at throwing shells into the sea. "This play is; to choose a shell from the shore, rubbed and made smooth by the tossing of the waves; to take hold of the shell in a horizontal position with the fingers; to whirl it along sloping and as low down as possible on the waves, that when thrown it may either skim the back of the wave, or may swim as it glides along with a smooth impulse, or may spring up as it cleaves the top of the waves, and rise as if lifted up with repeated springs. That boy claimed to be conqueror whose shell both went out furthest and leaped up most frequently."[1]

All this while Cœcilius was silent and sulky, and Minucius asks, "What is the matter? Why are you not so lively as usual?" The answer is, that he is nettled at Octavius' speech and indirect imputation of folly, and is anxious for an argument with him. He suggests that they seat themselves on the rocky barriers that are placed for the protection of the baths, and argue there. The suggestion is carried out, Minucius is placed in the middle as arbiter, and Cœcilius begins.

After reminding Minucius that, though a Christian, he as judge must hold the balance even, he begins by remarking that there is no difficulty in making plain that all human affairs are doubtful, uncertain, and unsettled, and that all things are rather probable than true. Such being the case, all men must be indignant that certain persons, and these unskilled in learning, and strangers to literature, and without knowledge of the common arts, should dare to determine with certainty matters on which different religions differed, and on which philosophy still deliberated. When you examine Creation, you cannot find its origin. When you observe events in the world, you can find no

[1] An ancient description of the English "duck and drake."

order or discrimination, and no distinction between the good and the bad. Fortune unrestrained by laws seems to be ruling over us. Under these circumstances it is better to receive the teaching of our ancestors, and to assert no opinion about the gods. Each people has its national rites of worship, and adores its local gods. The Romans, adoring all divinities, have conquered all nations. Their wars have always been religious. When conquered at home, they still worshipped the gods who had not taken care of them; when conquerors abroad, they venerated the conquered deities. In all directions they seek for the gods of the strangers and make them their own. Experience has shown that this devotion is expedient. This attention to religion has given prosperity. Neglected auguries have brought with them disaster. The philosophers are not, therefore, to be listened to when they strive to undermine a religion so ancient, so useful, and so wholesome. Much less is it to be tolerated that men of a reprobate, and unlawful, and desperate faction, gathered from the lowest dregs of the people, leagued together by nightly meetings and inhuman rites, a people skulking and shunning the light, should rage against the gods. This wicked confederacy grows daily, and assuredly ought to be rooted out and execrated. Its worship is secret, by report abominable, certainly suspicious. Unless it was vile, why do its followers conceal it so carefully? Why have they no altars, no temples or acknowledged images..

Proceeding to discuss Christian doctrines, The Providence of God extending over each and all, The destruction by fire of the eternal order constituted by the Divine laws of nature, The resurrection of the body after it has been resolved into dust, are marked out by Cœcilius as specially foolish. He argues that the present condition of the Christians is a sufficient proof of the vanity of their hopes. The greater part of them are in want and cold, and their God suffers it. Why? Because he is either unwilling or unable to assist his people. Those who dream of immortality are shaken by danger, consumed by fever, and torn by pain. Yes, and they have special troubles. For them were threats, punishments, fines, and crosses not for adoration,[1] but for torture. Who was that God who was able to bring them to life again, when He was unable to help them whilst in life? Of all men they were the most miserable in life, and there was nothing beyond. Cease, Cœcilius exhorts them in conclusion, to pry into the regions of the sky. All matters relating to the gods are uncertain, and had far better be left as we find them. And now Cœcilius has talked himself out of his temper, and exults in the prospect of a decided victory; but Minucius asks him to restrain his self-approval till he has heard the other side.

Octavius, in his reply, first remarks on the doubtful position of his opponent, at one time believing the gods, at another quite doubtful on the subject. He answers the objection brought against the Christians as illiterate, poor, unskilled people, by remarking that wisdom is not obtained by wealth, but implanted by

---

[1] For the allusion here, see page 47; Octavius replies, ' Crosses we neither worship nor wish for."

nature. It is quite true that man ought to know himself, and should study the works of nature. But when you lift up your eyes to heaven, and look into the things below and around, what can possibly be more evident than that there is some God of most excellent intelligence by whom all nature is inspired, moved, nourished, and governed? The movements of the stars in the heavens, and the order of the seasons upon earth, the ebbs and flows of the tides, and the perpetual flowing of the fountains and rivers, the varied faculties of the animals, and, above all, men, with their body of upright stature, and many members all beautiful and necessary, all having the same general form, and yet so unlike in special features,—all these need a Supreme Artificer and perfect Intelligence to create, to fashion, and to arrange them.

Proceeding to show that God's care is manifestly exerted, not only over the whole universe, but over its several parts, he makes a remark specially interesting to us: "Britain," he says, "is deficient in sunshine, but is refreshed by the warmth of the sea that flows around it." The house of the world, he argues, being thus beautiful and well-ordered, the Lord of the house must be far greater and more glorious. The analogy of the history of the world shows that that Lord is one; the authority of the Divine empire cannot be sundered. Such is God's greatness that He is incomprehensible, and so a name cannot be given Him. Nor is this necessary. Being unique, He needs not to be distinguished from others by a name. All these truths are confirmed by the discourse of the common people, and the testimonies of poets and the wisest philosophers. Why, then, should men be carried away by the errors of their credulous ancestors?

Going into detail, Octavius shows the human origin of the gods, the ridiculous and corrupting character of their history and their rites of worship. He dissociates Roman prosperity from Roman religion. He shows that the oracles were unreliable, and traces their power to the demons. He claims that the demons are subject to the powers of the Christians. He rebuts the accusations of immorality and unworthy and infamous objects of worship; and he contrasts the lives of Christians with those of heathens.

Not by a small bodily mark, as Cœcilius had supposed, are Christians distinguished, but very plainly by the sign of innocency and modesty. They love one another, because they do not know how to hate. They call one another brethren, because they are born of one God and Parent, because they are companions in faith, and co-heirs in hope.

Nor again is it for purposes of concealment that they have no temples, and altars, and images. Image of God there can be none, except man. Temple of God cannot be built, since the world itself cannot contain Him. The sacrifices to be offered to God are not sheep and cattle—His own gift to men; but a good soul, and a pure mind, and a sincere judgment. Certainly the God whom Christians worship, they can neither show nor see. We cannot even look upon or into His works, how then can we look upon Himself? And yet He is not far away and ignorant of men's doings. All things are full of Him. We live under His eyes, and even in His bosom.

After showing the possibility of a dissolution of all things, and adducing the argument from analogy which nature gives to the doctrine of the resurrection, he points out that God permits suffering as a trial and discipline. God's soldier is neither forsaken in suffering, nor brought to an end by death. The Christian may seem to be miserable, but is not really so. Those only are truly wretched who know not God. Apart from the knowledge of God, what solid happiness can there be, since death must come? Like a dream, happiness slips away before it is grasped. The Christians use this world as not abusing it, and have their innocent enjoyments here; but they live in contemplation of the future, and are animated by the hope of future happiness.

When Octavius ceases to speak there is silence for a time, and then Cœcilius breaks forth: "I do not wait for the decision. We are both conquerors; Octavius has conquered me, and I have conquered error. I yield to God. I have many questions yet to ask, not in a spirit of doubt but of inquiry."

After a few words from Minucius, all separate, glad and cheerful. Cæcilius, to rejoice that he had believed; Octavius, to rejoice that he had conquered; and Minucius, the friend of both, to rejoice for both reasons alike.

CYPRIAN. 200–258 A.D.

Cyprian's life was momentous in its issues, but his Apologetic treatises are short, and of no great importance, and are, in part, derived from the writings of former Apologists. His address to Demetrian, proconsul of Africa, contains a remarkable description of the sufferings the Christians had to endure: "You deprive," he says, "the innocent, the just, the dear to God, of their home; you spoil them of their estate, you load them with chains, you shut them up in prison, you punish them with the sword, with the wild beasts, with the flames. Nor, indeed, are you content that we should have a brief endurance of suffering, and a simple and swift exhaustion of pains. You set on foot tedious tortures, by tearing our bodies; you multiply numerous punishments, by lacerating our vitals; nor can your brutality and fierceness be content with ordinary tortures. Your ingenious cruelty devises new sufferings. Why," he asks, "do you turn your attention to the weakness of our body? Why do you strive with the feebleness of this earthly flesh? Contend rather with the strength of the mind; break down the power of the soul; destroy our faith; conquer, if you can, by discussion; overcome by reason; or, if your gods have any deity and power, let them themselves rise to their own vindication, let them defend themselves by their own majesty." He goes on to show that the heathen gods are all unable to protect themselves. They are the demons whom the Christians cast out. "Oh, would you but hear and see them when they are adjured by us, and are tortured with spiritual scourges, and are ejected from the possessed bodies with torture of words, when, howling and groaning at the voice of man and the power of God, feeling the stripes and blows, they confess the judgment to come! Come and acknowledge that what we say is true; and since you say that you thus worship gods, believe even those whom you worship; or, if you will even believe yourself, he (*i.e.* the demon) who has now possessed your breast, who has now darkened your mind with the night of ignorance, shall speak concerning yourself in your hearing; you will see that we are entreated by those whom you entreat, that we are feared by those whom you fear, and whom you adore; you will see that under our hands they stand bound and tremble as captives, whom you look up to and venerate as lords; assuredly, even thus you might be confounded in those errors of yours, when you see and hear gods, at once, upon our interrogation, betraying what they are, and even in your presence unable to conceal these deceits and trickeries of theirs."

The claim which Cyprian here makes is a very remarkable one; and he is not alone in making it. Every Apologist, with one exception (Clement of Alexandria), asserts that the power of casting out devils was a power continuing in, and being constantly exercised by, the Christian Church. Tertullian is quite ready to rest the Christian cause on the result of the encounter of any Christian with any demoniac.

ARNOBIUS. 300 A.D. CIRCA.

Arnobius's Apology is of great value. His rhetorical power was great. He wrote from the standpoint of an unbeliever, for he was not yet admitted into the Christian Church, and was evidently still ignorant of many of her doctrines.[1] A professor of rhetoric at Sicca, in Africa, he had been active in his attacks on Christianity, and devoted in his worship of images. When he wished to become a Christian (led by visions, Jerome tells us), his sincerity was at first suspected, and he composed his Apology as a pledge of his good faith. Amongst all the Apologists he is able most clearly to distinguish the Christian and the heathen miracles. His exposure of heathenism contains passages of scathing, though somewhat too redundant, eloquence. Many of these have been already quoted in a compressed form.

Inasmuch as Christianity was well known when Arnobius wrote, he naturally touches on matters which had not been noticed by former Apologists. The writings of the New Testament were in heathen hands, and they were objected to as containing barbarisms and solecisms. Arnobius asks how the truth of the substance is affected by the roughness of the form. The Christians discuss matters far removed from mere display; and they consider how they may benefit their hearers, not how they may tickle their ears.

He discusses at great length the nature of the soul. He denies that it is immortal, or that it comes

---

[1] Jerome, Cat. Script. Ecc., Arn. i. 39.

direct from God. If it were born of God, men's lives would be pure, and their beliefs one and the same. He thinks that naturally a man does not differ in kind from the animals. He suggests an experiment to prove his point. He supposes an infant brought up in a place where no sound or cry, no beast or bird, no storm or man, ever comes. He is to be tended by a dumb nurse, and to be fed on an invariable vegetable diet. He is to drink no wine, but only water from the spring. Thus he is to pass his life for twenty or thirty years, and then he is to be brought into the assemblies of men and questioned who and what he is. Will he not stand speechless, with less wit and sense than any beast, ignorant of the names and natures of the things offered to him? Arnobius thinks that you have here a man in his natural condition, and that his utter ignorance shows that his soul cannot have a divine origin. Of course, the fallacy of his argument lies here, that faculties, if uneducated and undeveloped, are wholly lost. Arnobius took care to preserve the bodily life of his infant with food, he left the soul unprovided with food, and it necessarily perished.

In his seventh book he has an elaborate argument against material sacrifices. He wants to know for what reason they are offered. Are the gods of heaven nourished by them? Surely not, since they are immortal. Moreover, the substance of the sacrifice is not consumed by them, but by fire. What pleasure can the gods above take in the slaughter of harmless creatures? Even we, half savage men, take some pity when we see the victims bleeding. They are offered, men say, that the gods may lay aside their anger. But can passion be felt by the Deity? If it can, why should the killing of a pig, or the consuming of a pullet, or the blood of a goose, or a goat, or a peacock, bring them relief? Are the gods like little boys, who give up their fits of passion when gifts of sparrows, or dolls, or ponies, are made to them? Then again, why should the burden of men's sins be cast on the innocent animals? He pictures an ox addressing Jupiter, and saying, that he had never done him wrong, or celebrated his games irreverently, or polluted his sacred groves. Man was the cause of all wickedness, why then should he (an ox) be slain to soothe the divine anger? Again, Arnobius objects, does not experience show that the sacrifices are of no avail for procuring benefits? Is it not dishonouring to the gods to suppose that their gifts are an object of sale, to be purchased by rich scoundrels, beyond the reach of the pious if poor? The gods, though not benefited, are honoured by the sacrifices, it is said. What! honoured by that foul smell which is emitted by burning hides, by bones, by bristles, by the fleeces of lambs, and the feathers of fowls! What kind of honour is it to invite a god to a banquet of blood, which he shares with dogs? What kind of honour is it to set on fire piles of wood, to hide the heavens with smoke, to darken with gloomy blackness the images of the gods? If dogs and asses, and swallows, and pigs were to offer sacrifices to you, how would you like it? Supposing the swallows consecrated flies to you, and the asses put hay upon your altars and poured out libations of chaff; supposing that the dogs placed bones on your altars, and the pigs poured out a horrid mess from their troughs, would you not be inflamed with rage? And then your sacrificial laws by which you offer different animals to different gods, how destitute of reason are they? Why do you offer a bull's blood to Jupiter, and a goat to Bacchus, and a barren heifer to Proserpine? In a similar manner he exposes the folly of offering wine to the gods, as if they could be thirsty, and he shows how utterly impossible it is that they can take delight in the shameless games which are celebrated in their honour. He traces all these vicious opinions to this cause :—Men were unable to know what God is, they were unable to discern Him by the power of reason, and so they fashioned gods for themselves and like themselves.

LACTANTIUS. 250–325 A.D.

Lactantius's 'Divine Institutions' was written when persecution had ceased. In the latter part of his work he goes quite beyond the Apologetic limits. His object was a very ambitious one. It was so to plead the Christian cause, as not only to overthrow former writers against it with all their writings, but also to cut off from future writers the whole power of writing and of replying. With one blow he hopes to overthrow all accusers of righteousness. He only asks for attention (v. 4), and then he will assuredly effect that man must either embrace Christian doctrine, or at least cease to deride it. He compares his work with that of other Apologists. Tertullian sought only to answer accusers, he seeks to instruct. Cyprian did not handle his subject as he ought, for he endeavoured to refute his adversaries by testimonies from Scripture which they did not admit, instead of by arguments and reason (v. 4). He intends to use the testimonies of philosophers and historians. There have been wanting amongst us, he says (v. 1), suitable and skilful teachers, who might vigorously and sharply refute public errors, and who might defend the whole cause of truth with elegance and copiousness. Tertullian had little readiness of speech, was not sufficiently polished, and was very obscure. He undertakes to plead the cause of truth with distinctness and elegance of speech, in order that it may flow with greater power into the minds of men, being both provided with its own force, and adorned with brilliancy of speech (i. 1).

If we had no other evidence than this criticism of former Apologists, and this self-complacent application of his own powers, we should, I think, be justified in assuming that the Apologetic period had nearly come to an end, and that Christians were no longer struggling for existence. Lactantius falls into some of the errors which he points out in others. If he is more eloquent, he is less forcible than some of those who had gone before. The most interesting part of his work is his refutation of Philosophy. He has a clear idea of the nature and causes of its failure, and he does not refuse to give it credit for that which it had been able to achieve. His work is not a defence of Christians from accusations; he defends them, indeed, from the charge of foolishness, but does not refer to any charges of immorality or impiety. Christianity was much better known than in the first Apologists' time. The ground was cleared for a work like the 'Divine Institutions,' which should discuss in greater detail the nature and evidence of a religion which had, single-handed, fought a battle against the Roman State, and won a complete victory.

CONCLUSION.

And now our task is complete. We cannot sum up our results better than in the noble words of an unknown Apologist.[1]

"The Christians are distinguished from other men, neither by country, nor language, nor the customs which they observe. For they neither inhabit cities of their own, nor employ a peculiar form of speech, nor lead a life which is marked out by any singularity. Their course of conduct has not been devised by any speculation of inquisitive men; nor do they proclaim themselves the advocates of any merely human doctrine. Inhabiting, as lot may determine, Greek as well as barbarian cities, following the customs of the natives with respect to clothing, food, and other matters, they display to us their wonderful and confessedly paradoxical mode of life. They dwell in their own countries, but simply as sojourners. As citizens, they share all things with others, and yet endure all things as aliens. Every foreign land is to them as their native country, and every land of their

[1] Author of Epistle to Diognetus, c. 5, 6.

birth as a land of strangers. They marry, as do all others, and beget children, but they do not destroy their offspring. They have a common table, but not an impure one. They are in the flesh, but they do not live after the flesh. They pass their days on earth, but they are citizens of heaven. They obey the prescribed laws, and at the same time surpass the laws by their lives. They love all men, and are persecuted by all. They are unknown and condemned; they are put to death, and restored to life. They are poor, yet make many rich; they are in lack of all things, and yet abound in all; they are dishonoured, and yet in their very dishonour are glorified. They are evil spoken of, and yet are justified; they are reviled, and bless; they are insulted, and repay the insult with honour; they do good, yet are punished as evil-doers. When punished, they rejoice as if quickened into life. They are assailed by the Jews as foreigners, and are persecuted by the Greeks; and yet those who hate them are unable to assign any reason for their hatred. To sum up all in one word; what the soul is in the body, that are the Christians in the world. The soul is dispersed through all the members of the body, and Christians are dispersed through all the cities of the world. The soul dwells in the body, yet is not of the body; and Christians dwell in the world, yet are not of the world. The invisible soul is guarded by the visible body; and Christians are indeed known to be in the world, but their godliness remains invisible. The flesh hates the soul, and wars against it, though itself suffering no injury, because it is prevented from enjoying pleasures. The world, also, hates the Christians, though in no wise injured, because they abjure pleasures. The soul loves the flesh that hates it, and loves also the members; Christians likewise love those that hate them. The soul is imprisoned in the body, yet preserves that very body; and Christians are confined in the world as in a prison, and yet they are the preservers of the world. The immortal soul dwells in a mortal tabernacle; and Christians dwell as sojourners in corruptible bodies, looking for an incorruptible dwelling in the heavens. The soul, when but ill provided with food and drink, becomes better; in like manner, the Christians, though subjected day by day to punishment, increase the more in number. God has assigned them this illustrious position, which it were unlawful for them to forsake." How had all this come to pass? No mere "earthly invention" or "human system of opinion" had been committed to them, but truly "God Himself had sent from heaven and placed among men, Him who is the Truth, and the holy and incomprehensible Word, and had firmly established Him in their hearts. He did not, as might have been supposed, send to men any servant, or angel, or ruler in heaven or earth, but the very Creator and Fashioner of all things. Did He send Him for the purpose of exercising tyranny, or inspiring fear? By no means; but in clemency and meekness. As the king sends his son, so sent He Him. As God, He sent Him; as to men, He sent Him: as a Saviour, He sent Him. As calling us, not vengefully pursuing us, as loving us, not judging us, He sent Him. He will yet send Him to judge us, and who shall endure His appearing? Do you not see (the Christians) exposed to wild beasts, that they may be persuaded to deny the Lord, and yet not overcome? Do you not see that the more of them are punished, the greater becomes the number of the rest? This does not seem to be the work of men. THIS IS THE POWER OF GOD."

FINIS.

PUBLICATIONS

OF THE

Society for Promoting Christian Knowledge.

Most of these Works may be had in Ornamental Bindings, with Gilt Edges, at a small extra charge.

                                                                            Price.
                                                                                s. d.

Adventures of Marshall Vavasour, Midshipman.
With three full-page illustrations on toned paper. Crown 8vo .... *cloth boards* 1 6

Africa Unveiled.
By the Rev. H. ROWLEY. With Map, and eight full-page illustrations on toned paper. Crown 8vo *cloth boards* 5 0

An Eventful Night, and What came of it.
Adapted from the German of Ernst Andolt. With three page illustrations. Fcap. 8vo .... *cloth boards* 1 0

Australia's Heroes:
Being a slight Sketch of the most prominent amongst the band of gallant men who devoted their lives and energies to the cause of Science, and the development of the fifth Continent. By CHARLES H. EDEN, Esq., Author of "Home of the Wolverene and Beaver," &c. With Map. Crown 8vo .... *cloth boards* 5 0

China: The Land and the People of.
A short Account of the Geography, History, Religion, Social Life, Arts, Industries, and Government of China and its People. By J. THOMSON, Esq., F.R.G.S., With Map, and twelve full-page illustrations on toned paper. Crown 8vo .... *cloth boards* 5 0

Drifted Away.
A Tale of Adventure. With three full-page illustrations on toned paper. Crown 8vo .... *cloth boards* 2 6

Fan: a Village Tale.
With two full-page illustrations on toned paper. Crown 8vo .... *cloth boards* 1 0

Fifth Continent (The), with the adjacent Islands.
Being an Account of Australia, Tasmania, and New Guinea, with Statistical Information to the latest date. By CHARLES H. EDEN, Author of "Australia's Heroes," &c. With Map. Crown 8vo .... *cloth boards* 5 0

      1-11-77.]   [Fcap. 8vo.

Price.
s. d.

For Faith and Fatherland.
By M. BRAMSTON, Author of "Rosamond Ferrars," &c. With three full-page illustrations on toned paper. Crown 8vo.. *cloth boards* 2 6

Girls of Bredon (The); and Manor House Stories.
By Mrs. STANLEY LEATHES. With three full-page illustrations on toned paper. Crown 8vo... *cloth boards* 2 0

Great Captain (The): An eventful Chapter in Spanish History.
By ULICK R. BURKE, M.A. With two full-page illustrations on toned paper. Crown 8vo..........*cloth boards* 2 0

Heroes of the Arctic and their Adventures.
By FREDERICK WHYMPER, Esq., Author of "Travels in Alaska." With Map, eight full-page illustrations and numerous small woodcuts. Crown 8vo ......*cloth boards* 5 0

Heroes of the North; or, Stories from Norwegian Chronicle.
By F. SCARLETT POTTER, Esq. With three full-page illustrations on toned paper. Crown 8vo ... *cloth boards* 2 6

Home of the Wolverene and Beaver (The); or, Fur-hunting in the Wilds of Canada.
By C. H. EDEN, Esq., Author of "Australia's Heroes," &c. With three full-page illustrations on toned paper. Crown 8vo.. *cloth boards* 2 6

In and Out of London; or, The Half-Holidays of a Town Clerk.
By the Rev. W. J. LOFTIE, B.A., Author of "A Century of Bibles," &c. With four full-page illustrations and numerous small engravings. Post 8vo ...... *cloth boards* 2 6

In the Marsh.
By Miss B. C. CURTEIS. With three full-page illustrations on toned paper. Crown 8vo .... *cloth boards* 2 6

King's Namesake (The).
A Tale of Carisbrooke Castle. By CATHERINE MARY PHILLIMORE. With four full-page illustrations on toned paper. Crown 8vo .... *cloth boards* 2 0

London Sparrows.
By the Author of "Ruth Lee," &c. With three full-page illustrations on toned paper. Crown 8vo *cloth boards* 1 6

Marchfield: a Story of Commercial Morality.
By the Author of "In and Out of London," &c. With three full-page illustrations on toned paper. Crown 8vo *cloth boards* 2 6

FOR PROMOTING CHRISTIAN KNOWLEDGE.

Price.
s. d.

Michael Penguyne; or, Fisher Life on the Cornish Coast.
By W. H. G. KINGSTON, Esq. With three full-page illustrations on toned paper. Crown 8vo ... *cloth boards* 1 6

Our Valley.
By the Author of "The Children of Seeligsberg," &c. With three full-page illustrations on toned paper. Crown 8vo. .... *cloth boards* 2 6

Owen Hartley; or, Ups and Downs.
A Tale of the Land and Sea. By William H. G. KINGSTON, Esq., Author of "The Settlers," &c. &c. With five full-page illustrations on toned paper. Crown 8vo.. *cloth boards* 2 6

Panelled House (The): a Chronicle of Two Sisters' Lives.
By M. BRAMSTON. With three illustrations on toned paper. Crown 8vo .... *cloth boards* 3 6

Postmaster of Prenzlau (The), and other Tales.
From the German. With two page woodcuts, on toned paper. Crown 8vo................................ *cloth boards* 1 6

Seppi.
Adapted from the German of Franz Hoffmann. By M. MONTGOMERIE CAMPBELL. With three page illustrations. Fcap. 8vo. .... *cloth boards* 1 6

Shepherd of Ardmuir (The).
With three full-page illustrations on toned paper. Crown 8vo.. *cloth boards* 2 6

Silent Jim: a Cornish Story.
By JAMES F. COBB, Esq., Author of "A Tale of Two Brothers," &c. With four full-page illustrations on toned paper. Crown 8vo .... *cloth boards* 3 6

Snowball Society (The): a Story for Children.
By M. BRAMSTON, Author of "Rosamond Ferrars," &c. &c. With three full-page illustrations on toned paper. Crown 8vo. ....*cloth boards* 2 6

Snow Fort and the Frozen Lake (The); or, Christmas Holidays at Pond House.
By EADGYTH. With three full-page illustrations on toned paper. Crown 8vo........................ *cloth boards* 2 6

Stories from Italian History.
By B. MONTGOMERIE RANKING. With two full-page illustrations on toned paper. Crown 8vo.... *cloth boards* 1 6

PUBLICATIONS OF THE SOCIETY.

Price.
s. d.

Two Voyages, and What came of them.
By the Author of "A Child of the Glens," "Motherless Maggie," &c. With three full-page illustrations on toned paper. Crown 8vo .... *cloth boards*   2   0

Walter Campbell; or, The Chorister's Reward.
By the Author of "Ellen Mansel," &c. With three page illustrations. 18mo. .... *cloth boards*   1   0

Wreath of Mallow (The), and other Stories more or less true.
By Mrs. JEROME MERCIER. With three page woodcuts, on toned paper. Crown 8vo .... *cloth boards*   2   0

New Series of 3s. 6d. Books.

Post 8vo, with Coloured Frontispiece and Title, Four Full-page Woodcuts, and numerous small Engravings.

A Cruise on the Bosphorus, and in the Marmora and Ægean Seas.
By the Rev. G. FYLER TOWNSEND, M.A., Author of "The Sea Kings," "Siege of Colchester," &c.

Away on the Moorland: a Highland Tale.
By A. C. CHAMBERS, Author of "Robin the Bold," &c.

Julian's Dream: a Story of A.D. 362.
By the Rev. GERALD S. DAVIES, Author of "Gaudentius," &c.

Rosamond Ferrars.
By M. BRAMSTON, Author of "The Panelled House," &c.

The Settlers: a Tale of Virginia.
By W. H. G. KINGSTON, Esq., Author of "The Two Shipmates," "Michael Penguyne," &c.

Two Campaigns: a Tale of Old Alsace.
By A. H. ENGELBACH, Esq., Author of "Lionel's Revenge," &c.

Depositories:

77, GREAT QUEEN STREET, LINCOLN'S-INN FIELDS;
4, ROYAL EXCHANGE; 48, PICCADILLY;
AND BY ALL BOOKSELLERS.

www.ingramcontent.com/pod-product-compliance
Lightning Source LLC
Chambersburg PA
CBHW031817220426
43662CB00007B/684